ideas for great fireplaces

By Cynthia Bix and
the Editors of Sunset Books

Menlo Park, California

Sunset Books

vice president, general manager:
Richard A. Smeby

vice president, editorial director:
Bob Doyle

production director:
Lory Day

director of operations:
Rosann Sutherland

retail sales development manager:
Linda Barker

executive editor:
Bridget Biscotti Bradley

art director:
Vasken Guiragossian

special sales:
Brad Moses

Staff for this book:

developmental editor:
Linda J. Selden

copy editor:
Phyllis Elving

photo director/stylist:
JoAnn Masaoka Van Atta

principal photographer:
Jamie Hadley

illustrator:
Beverley Bozarth Colgan

page production:
Linda M. Bouchard

prepress coordinator:
Danielle Javier

proofreader:
Mary Roybal

10 9 8 7 6 5 4
First printing June 2004
*Copyright © 2004 Sunset Publishing Corporation,
Menlo Park, CA 94025. First edition. All rights reserved,
including the right of reproduction in whole or in part
in any form.*

ISBN 0-376-01760-0
Library of Congress Control Number: 2004101210
Printed in the United States.

*For additional copies of Ideas for Great Fireplaces or
any other Sunset book, visit our web site at www.sunset.com
or call 1-800-526-5111.*

*Cover main image: Harvey Mathistad of HM Custom Homes,
builder; Timothy Schouten, David Giulietti, and Michelle Schultz,
architects; Jan Kavale, interior designer; photography by David
Wakely. Top left: photography by Michael Skott. Top middle:
photography by Jamie Hadley. Top right: photography by Brian
Vanden Brink. Cover design: Vasken Guiragossian.*

By the fireside

No matter where you live—in a lakeside cottage or an urban loft, a contemporary showplace or a vintage home with historic charm—there's a place for the delights of the fireside. In this book, you'll learn about fireplaces and stoves of every kind, from traditional masonry ones to high-tech prefab models, from environmentally friendly wood stoves to European thermal heaters. Practical information and photos galore will help you find the right solution for your living situation.

We are grateful to the many professionals who shared their expertise with us and to the homeowners who generously allowed us to photograph their fireplaces and stoves. We'd especially like to thank Don Smith of Okell's Fireplace in San Francisco, California, for his valuable advice, and Okell's for accommodating our photography team. Special thanks, also, to Sally McKnight of The Irish Sweep in Alameda, California, and to Peter Solac of Woodland Stoves & Fireplaces in Minneapolis, Minnesota. In addition, we thank Bob Gau of Woodland Stoves & Fireplaces in Minneapolis; Mark Shubatt of The Firebird in Santa Fe, New Mexico; Ronald Mazzeo of Mazzeo's Stoves & Fireplaces in Rockport, Maine; and FoxFire in Grass Valley, California. For architects and designers whose work is featured in photographs, turn to pages 126–127.

contents

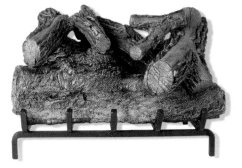

all kinds of hearths

EVER SINCE THE FIRST FIRES were built in primitive shelters to ward off the cold and darkness, the warmth of flames dancing on a hearth has been a primal source of comfort and safety. In every age and in every part of the world, people have made a hearth the center of their homes—for heating, for cooking, and for gathering together. And over the years, as dwellings became increasingly elaborate, their owners devised ever more beautiful and varied ways to contain and frame their fires—with stone and wood, tile and copper.

Even in today's high-tech, urban world, the lure of the fireplace is compelling. According to recent statistics gathered by the remodeling and real estate industries, a fireplace is one of the most popular features sought by people when buying a home. Adding a fireplace or stove to an existing home can add to its value.

Thanks to new fireplace and stove technologies, materials, and designs, there are more fireside possibilities than ever before. You can choose a traditional wood-burning fireplace built of sturdy stone and brick, or you can opt for a heat-efficient, environmentally friendly prefabricated fireplace or stove that can be fueled by gas, wood pellets, or even electricity. Select a freestanding European fireplace designed to deliver radiant heat throughout your house, or install a sleekly contemporary wood stove. These days, you can have a fireplace just about anywhere in your home—from the living room to the kitchen to the bathroom—as well as outdoors, warming your patio or porch.

The handsome plaster fireplace at left hints at a traditional Spanish influence. Its unique surround features a double layer of plate steel with cutouts in the darker outer layer. Steel also caps the raised hearth. Plaster gives the fireplace a softly sculpted look.

Whether you're installing a fireplace or stove in a new home or addition or want to upgrade an existing fireplace, you'll find help in the following pages. The first section of this book, "Planning & Design," covers the basics—including fireplace and stove technologies, new and old. You'll even find pointers for upgrading your fireplace's appearance and for creative decorating on and around your fireplace. Then, in "A Gallery of Ideas," you'll gain inspiration from dozens of photographs showing all kinds of fireplaces and stoves, in all sorts of rooms. Finally, "A Shopper's Guide" offers a closer look at the options awaiting you when you begin shopping for your fireplace or stove and accessories.

In this gracious bungalow-style guest cottage, a stone fireplace with simple wood beam mantel looks right at home.

PLANNING & DESIGN

IN THIS INCREASINGLY URBAN, high-tech world, we still love to savor the ancient pleasures of the fireside. Today's fireplaces and stoves let us do just that, but they make use of modern ingenuity and—yes—technology to bring us the pleasures of the fireplace in new forms that are efficient, clean-burning, and flexible enough to go almost anywhere. THIS CHAPTER offers a brief overview of fireplace and stove technologies—traditional and new. You'll learn about options ranging from old-fashioned stone fireplaces to sleek enameled stoves, from high-tech gas fireplaces to simple portable outdoor fire pits. ON THE AESTHETIC SIDE of the equation, you'll find an exciting array of designs, as well as ideas to help you create a welcoming fireside living space around the fireplace or stove of your choice.

a matter of style

FIREPLACES OF ONE KIND *or another have been central features in dwellings of every era, in every part of the world, and in every stratum of society—from peasantry to royalty. From the simplest pioneer stone hearth and chimney to the most elaborate marble Baroque-period mantel and surround, the styles of fireplaces—and wood stoves—reflect both artistic and economic concerns of diverse people and places throughout history.*

Southwestern style is evident in the organic curves and the adobe-like material of this fireplace built into the corner of a covered patio.

Finding your style

You'll probably want to base the style of your own fireplace on the architectural style of your home's interior. Whether you choose to carry out that style in every detail or simply to capture the essence of it through materials or motifs, you'll want it to be compatible.

Architectural styles—and the fireplaces that go along with them—can be defined in many ways, from specific historic "periods" to broad categories like "Old World" or simply "traditional." An 18th-century Georgian fireplace with marble facing and classical motifs is an example of a particular period style. America's Arts and Crafts movement of the late 19th to early 20th centuries was a reaction to the fussiness of the earlier Victorian period, and Craftsman fireplaces typically featured substantial wood mantels with built-in bookcases or benches on either side.

Old World or European style takes in various possibilities—French country, Mediterranean, Spanish, and so on. Country-style Old World fireplaces are usually fashioned of stone or smooth plaster, often with tiled decoration and rustic wood mantels—designs that developed over centuries, shaped by available local materials and simple construction methods. In America, the distinctive kiva-style fireplace of the Southwest owes its rounded shape and native adobe material to Pueblo Indian tradition and technique, while its ceramic tile trim bespeaks a Spanish heritage as well.

"Traditional" style may conjure up images of an American Colonial brick fireplace with massive wood mantel and iron brackets for cooking, or a more formal Federal-style fireplace with symmetrically embellished mantel of polished wood. "Lodge" style suggests a rough-hewn rock fireplace with massive chimney and wide raised hearth, while "cottage" style may bring to mind anything from a simple wood mantel, painted white, to a wood stove of cheery red enamel. And a "contemporary" fireplace or stove will probably be sleek and sophisticated, featuring materials such as steel, glass, and concrete.

A traditional-looking fieldstone fireplace holds
a surprise—a very modern, prefabricated firebox.

FINDING HELP

Professional help in designing and installing your fireplace may come from a contractor who specializes in fireplaces, your fireplace dealer, an architect, or some combination of these. You may work with stock plans and components, or have them custom-designed and custom-made. Your architect or fireplace dealer may also help you select and work with masonry and fireplace contractors. Be sure to get references before signing contracts with any of these professionals.

Before conducting business with your professional help, do your homework. Search on the Internet and look through magazines and catalogs to get an idea of what styles, materials, and components appeal to you. Before you meet, gather as much as you can in the way of room dimensions, house layout, and other pertinent information.

STYLE SETTERS

The outer elements of a fireplace are what create its decorative style. These are the parts that make up a fireplace's exterior:

- **Mantel**—A shelf, beam, or other facing ornamentation mounted above and around the fireplace, usually made of wood, masonry, stone, or cast stone.

- **Surround**—The noncombustible facing ornamentation (also called the filler panel) mounted at the sides and top of the fireplace opening; this can be brick, tile, stone, or even stucco over metal mesh.

- **Hearth**—The area in front of the firebox opening, constructed of noncombustible material such as masonry or tile.

- **Overmantel**—The decorative facing that extends above the mantel of some fireplaces.

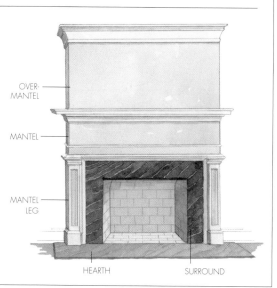

OVER-MANTEL

MANTEL

MANTEL LEG

HEARTH   SURROUND

A Scandinavian wood stove combines up-to-the-minute style with practical heating capability.

Style and substance

When you begin planning for a new or revamped fireplace, you'll actually be thinking about two aspects of the installation—the "working" component where the fire burns and the decorative elements that frame it, such as mantel, surround, and hearth. As you'll learn in the following pages, the firebox of a fireplace may be a traditional masonry version or it may be prefabricated (factory-built). When you take a casual look at a fireplace, you can't always tell what kind of firebox it has if you're not an expert.

But no matter what technology you choose, it's largely the design and materials of the surrounding elements that give the fireplace its particular style and character. These are what you'll be working with to integrate your fireplace into the interior style of your home. With a freestanding stove, it's the style of the appliance itself—its shape, color, and so forth—that makes a design statement.

Two very different looks are represented here: a tiled masonry fireplace (left) has classic Arts-and-Crafts styling, while a painted wood fireplace mantel (above) reproduces an 18th-century design.

planning & design

all the options

TO DECIDE AMONG *the many options available today for fireplaces and stoves, begin by identifying your own particular needs and wishes. Perhaps you want to upgrade an existing fireplace that functions inefficiently. Maybe you want an effective heat source as well as good looks—then you might choose an updated prefabricated version of a fireplace, a sophisticated European-style masonry heater, or a freestanding stove.*

Assessing your needs

Do you want a serious heat source, a special ambience, or both? Perhaps what you love is the coziness of a traditional fireplace. You may want a classic mantel and hearth to serve as a visual focal point and a gathering place. Maybe nothing will do but the aroma and crackle—the spark and dance—of a real wood fire. Then a conventional masonry fireplace, built to the most efficient standards possible, is for you. Of course, you must consider the practicalities: local building and air-quality regulations, the availability of firewood and a place to store it, the tasks of building and maintaining a fire, and cleanup and chimney maintenance chores.

A prefab fireplace with custom-designed concrete mantel and surround updates the traditional fireplace idea.

Perhaps you already have a wood-burning fireplace, but it's inefficient or non-functioning. You may want to upgrade it using some of the options discussed on pages 20–21. If your fireplace functions well but doesn't fit in with your decor, several ways to improve its looks are described on pages 22–25.

When it's a purely practical source of heat you're after, you'll want to consider a freestanding stove (wood, gas, or pellet) or a European masonry heater. You usually have lots of flexibility in placing a stove in your home, and new designs ensure good looks along with warmth.

If you're adding a fireplace as part of a remodel, your options are expanded. Various products are described on the following pages. Your choice will be influenced by aesthetics and also by factors such as location in your home. A lightweight prefabricated fireplace, for example, may be the perfect solution for an upstairs bedroom or a sitting room with no space for a traditional masonry chimney.

Fuel is an important factor—often the deciding one. For a discussion of the pros and cons of wood, gas, propane, pellets, gel fuel, and electricity, turn to pages 120–121.

On the following pages is an introduction to today's options. For more details, see "A Shopper's Guide," beginning on page 97.

HOW EFFICIENT?

Conventional wood-burning fireplaces vary in efficiency according to their inner configurations. The efficiency of any wood-burning fireplace or stove—how much of its combustion energy is turned into heat—is basically a function of how completely it burns the volatile gases and particulate matter that result from the combustion of wood. Smoke is actually unburned fuel particles. Even with a properly built and maintained fire, a traditional fireplace doesn't completely burn up all these particles.

Another factor in determining efficiency is how much heat goes up the chimney instead of into the room. With a conventional fireplace, much of the warm air escapes up the chimney, while cold air drafts flow down.

To learn more about fireplace pollution and efficiency, see "Clean Air Issues" on page 25.

With its graceful arched opening framed in ceramic tiles, this small wood-burning masonry fireplace is the embodiment of Old World distinction.

Masonry fireplaces

Traditional wood-burning fireplaces have a firebox and chimney built of brick or stone, adobe brick, or concrete. This makes them very heavy—up to 6 or 7 tons—so they require an extensive footing or foundation of masonry or poured concrete. For venting purposes, conventional masonry fireplaces have a masonry chimney extending above the roof line. A masonry fireplace must be constructed on-site by a qualified professional. Be aware that a conventional-style fireplace provides more ambience than actual heat.

The *Rumford fireplace* is a variation of the masonry fireplace developed by a Massachusetts scientist in the 18th century to radiate more heat into a room through the use of a shallow firebox and angled side walls. Contemporary redesigns have made this classic even more efficient. Rebuilding an existing fireplace in a Rumford configuration is one way to increase its efficiency.

ANATOMY OF A FIREPLACE

A traditional masonry fireplace rests on a reinforced concrete foundation and produces heat from a fire burning in a *firebox* built of heat-refractory firebrick. The firebox floor, the *inner hearth,* is also of firebrick; the *hearth extension* can be of brick, stone, or other non-combustible material.

A *lintel,* or metal bar, spans the top of the firebox opening and supports the decorative face of the fireplace. Behind or below the firebox in some fireplaces is an *ash pit*—a fireproof storage space where ashes are dumped for emptying through a clean-out door on the chimney exterior.

Above the firebox, the narrow *throat* opening lets hot air and smoke rise into the *smoke chamber.* A *damper*—a movable metal flap—blocks the throat when the fireplace isn't in use to keep warm indoor air from escaping up the chimney (and cold air from blowing in).

A symmetrically shaped, well-functioning smoke chamber is essential for creating a good draft to pull gases and smoke up the chimney. This is also where smoke recirculates so that remaining particles are more completely burned before they go up the chimney. A flat *smoke shelf* at the bottom of the smoke chamber collects soot that would otherwise fall back into the firebox.

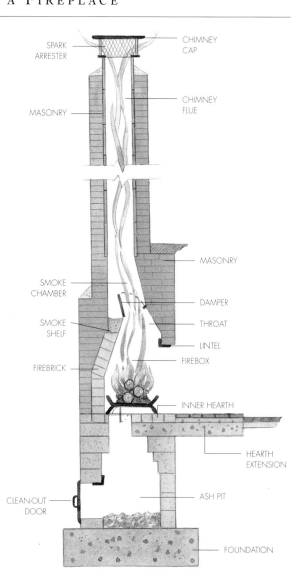

SPARK ARRESTER
CHIMNEY CAP
MASONRY
CHIMNEY FLUE
MASONRY
SMOKE CHAMBER
DAMPER
SMOKE SHELF
THROAT
FIREBRICK
LINTEL
FIREBOX
INNER HEARTH
CLEAN-OUT DOOR
HEARTH EXTENSION
ASH PIT
FOUNDATION

QUICK-START OPTION

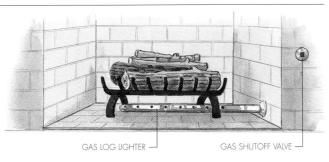

GAS LOG LIGHTER ┘   └ GAS SHUTOFF VALVE ┘

To speed up the process of starting a fire, a gas log lighter can be installed in the firebox of a masonry fireplace. You pile on wood and light the gas to produce instant flames.

Some masonry fireplaces have a double-walled, heavy-gauge steel firebox, with or without integral ducts for heat-circulating capability. These work by convection (see page 17); the vents are on the fireplace face.

FIREPLACE KITS. A relatively new technology has given rise to "kits" for fireplaces that mimic masonry fireplaces but are actually constructed of precast modular units of volcanic stone. This lightweight material insulates so well that it requires virtually no clearance between fireplace walls and combustible wood framing. The firebox is lined with standard firebrick, and the outside of the fireplace and chimney can be finished with whatever material you want. (These fireplaces can also be outfitted to burn gas or coal instead of wood.) These units offer the look of a traditional fireplace but with less weight and expense and greater heat output.

Other kits are more in the nature of construction guides for building masonry fireplaces. They may offer bolt-together steel frames along with factory-built blocks that can be assembled and finished by a mason.

Masonry heaters

Modified versions of a centuries-old European design, contemporary masonry heaters (also called thermal-mass or high-mass heaters) burn wood but extract heat differently than other wood-burners. These are the ultimate in radiant heating. Within a large masonry shell, heat generated in a small firebox during a short, very hot fire travels through a circuitous stone or metal channel to be absorbed by the surrounding

masonry, then slowly radiated out into the room over the following day or night.

Some masonry heaters are huge, site-built brick or stone fireplaces with efficient glass-doored metal fireboxes. Often, these are best positioned in the center of the house, so home construction must be planned around them.

Prefabricated masonry heaters made of soapstone (manufactured primarily in Scandinavia

Warmth stored up from a morning fire radiates all day long through the substantial soapstone walls of this prefabricated European freestanding fireplace.

A wood-burning fireplace insert has been artfully installed into an older masonry fireplace, transforming it into a good-looking yet practical source of real warmth.

but available in the United States) are still large and heavy, but they offer more flexibility of placement. Sometimes called freestanding or heat-storing fireplaces, they can be installed by a qualified professional in most rooms if there's sufficient structural support. Gas-fired and some electric models are available along with the traditional wood-fueled ones.

Fireplace inserts

An inefficient masonry fireplace can be substantially improved by having an insert installed. There are a number of different kinds of inserts, but all must go into a fireproof cavity such as a masonry firebox.

At the top of the list for efficiency are EPA-approved heavy metal inserts, usually lined with refractory brick. Whatever fuel they're designed to use (wood, pellets, gas, or even electricity), these function basically like freestanding stoves. Most have glass doors that allow fire-watching; some feature a blower to increase efficiency.

To install an insert, a properly sized chimney liner must be fitted inside the existing flue and attached to the top of the insert.

Simpler fireplace inserts include fan-driven heat exchangers, grate heaters that warm air in steel tubing, and gas-fueled ceramic "log" sets (see pages 104–105). Wood-burning or gas inserts are also available for some prefabricated fireboxes; ask your dealer about options.

Prefabricated fireplaces

Also called factory-built, manufactured, or zero-clearance fireplaces, these "new" alternatives to conventional fireplaces are the choice of more and more people. Prefabs feature a metal firebox (with or without ceramic brick lining) and a lightweight metal chimney, along with such components as chimney cap and flashing—all manufactured and sold as parts of a system.

Prefab fireplaces can be found in wood-burning, gas- or propane-fueled, and increasingly popular electric versions. Though some have an open hearth like a traditional fireplace, most are enclosed behind glass doors, increasing heat efficiency while allowing fire-viewing. Many employ convective heating—with or without blowers. Look for models that are EPA-certified to burn cleanly and efficiently.

Because they weigh much less than their masonry counterparts, prefabs often can be installed on an upper story without structural reinforcing. And unlike conventional fireplaces, they are "zero-clearance"—they usually require a minimum 1-inch clearance between the firebox and combustible materials such as wood framing. Electric models can be installed in an existing masonry fireplace or as a new fireplace, anywhere there's a 120-volt outlet.

Flexible venting options make prefabs easy to install in locations that might be problematic for traditional fireplaces. Wood-burning or gas-fired, they require only a simple metal chimney. Gas-fired prefabs may be direct-vent, B-vent, or vent-free (see page 100); make sure you understand the venting requirements, since they affect where you can locate the fireplace.

The long-term durability of prefabs hasn't been established. But lower installation costs and greater flexibility may offset that.

Alternative fireplaces

One kind of alternative fireplace is the freestanding wood-burning fireplace, prefabricated of metal and

A freestanding wood-burning fireplace (left) makes a cheery showcase for a fire. Be sure floor and wall surfaces around such units are noncombustible.

WARMING TRENDS

Fireplaces and stoves heat by either radiation or convection. The former is the direct transmission of energy in the form of infrared rays that heat objects they strike but not the air space in between. Traditional noncirculating fireplaces heat this way; that's why they're generally less effective as room heaters, though stoves or European masonry heaters can be very effective radiant heaters.

Convection is the movement of heat through air or fluids. Heated air rises, setting up convective currents that circulate the air. Convective fireplaces or stoves, which employ vents to draw in cool room air and circulate heated air back into the room, give off as much heat as radiant types but add circulating air warmed by convection. Referred to as "heat-circulating," these units feature double or triple walls, or sometimes tubes through which air is drawn and warmed. Many include electric blowers for added effectiveness.

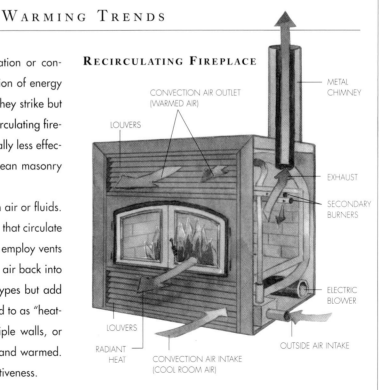

RECIRCULATING FIREPLACE

CONVECTION AIR OUTLET (WARMED AIR)

LOUVERS

METAL CHIMNEY

EXHAUST

SECONDARY BURNERS

ELECTRIC BLOWER

OUTSIDE AIR INTAKE

LOUVERS

RADIANT HEAT

CONVECTION AIR INTAKE (COOL ROOM AIR)

usually drum-shaped or roughly spherical. An opening on one side provides a view of the fire; the metal chimney is similar to that of free-standing stoves. These appliances work best if located so heat can radiate to all parts of a room; some have a refractory brick lining to radiate heat after the fire is out. They are not necessarily EPA-approved and are not approved for use in some places.

Another type of freestanding fireplace is designed to burn gel fuel (see page 121). Some of these look just like small conventional fireplaces. You can set gel fireplaces down virtually anywhere, but because they are vent-free, they must be used with extreme care in a well-ventilated room, and never in a bedroom. There are also outdoor models.

Today's stoves make good-looking additions to any home. Cases in point are the perky cranberry-red pellet stove at right and the handsome, easy-to-maintain gas stove below.

Freestanding stoves

The term "wood stove" may bring to mind the cast-iron, pot-bellied models found in old-time general stores. But think again—these days, wood stoves are sleek additions to almost any contemporary-style home.

What's more, new technology has made these the cleanest, most efficient wood-burners around. And many stoves are being designed to burn pellets—a fuel substitute for wood—or to be fueled by gas or electricity (see page 108). All wood stoves are required to meet EPA standards for clean burning, as described on page 25.

Made of steel or cast iron, with or without enamel or soapstone applied over it, freestanding stoves come in a variety of attractive finishes and colors to suit—or suggest—your decor. Styles range from period-specific (such as Victorian or Shaker) to thoroughly contemporary. Most freestanding stoves have glass doors that allow you to view your fire. They are vented to the outdoors through a metal chimney (some gas models are ventless—see page 100). Except for electric types, most require minimum clearances from combustible walls as well as a hearth pad or heatproof platform.

Extremely efficient and clean-burning, pellet-burning stoves surpass EPA requirements. Some can be rear-vented and don't require a full chimney. They do require electricity to power their auger and fan mechanisms.

STOVES THAT BURN TWICE

EPA-certified wood-burning prefab fireplaces, stoves, and inserts manufactured today usually use either *catalytic* or *noncatalytic* technology to burn cleanly by consuming volatile gases and particulates that would ordinarily escape into the air.

Catalytic combustors, made of a ceramic material coated with platinum or palladium, are located between firebox and chimney flue. They work much like the devices used to control car emissions. Units with catalytic combustors offer lower emissions, greater efficiency, larger fireboxes, and longer burn times than their noncatalytic wood-burning counterparts, but they can be more expensive, and the combustor may need to be replaced after three to six years.

Noncatalytic or "high-tech" stoves rely on a more sophisticated design, increased insulation, and additional air sources to create a secondary burn for particulates and gases. Their lively flames are pleasant to view, and they offer slightly lower cost compared to catalytic stoves, as well as easy maintenance and operation.

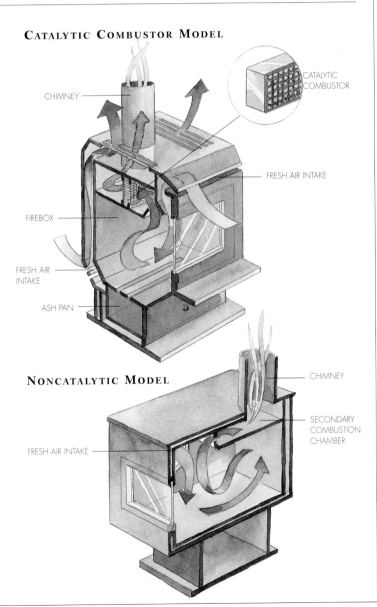

CATALYTIC COMBUSTOR MODEL

CHIMNEY

CATALYTIC COMBUSTOR

FRESH AIR INTAKE

FIREBOX

FRESH AIR INTAKE

ASH PAN

NONCATALYTIC MODEL

CHIMNEY

SECONDARY COMBUSTION CHAMBER

FRESH AIR INTAKE

Upgrading your fireplace

If you have a masonry fireplace that's smoky or drafty—or just plain falling apart—there are a number of ways to increase its efficiency and bring it into closer compliance with clean-air regulations. Seek professional help, have a clear understanding of local building codes, and find out about any chimney changes needed to go along with your upgrade.

If you want to continue burning wood, your first step should be to call in a professional chimney sweep or fireplace expert to evaluate your fireplace and chimney. To correct problems such as smoking, for example, it may be recommended that you alter the size of your fireplace opening, reconfigure the existing firebox, or add a chimney cap.

If lots of warm air is escaping up your chimney, the damper may be loose—or nonexistent. You can have a professional install a top-sealing damper. Glass doors will also help keep warm air from going up the chimney and cold air from flowing in; some locales *require* them in new or remodeled fireplaces. (Be sure to follow the manufacturer's directions for using the doors.)

Replacing your old grate or fire basket (the metal device that supports burning logs) can help. Some new grate designs improve air circulation and allow better log positioning. Hollow steel heat-exchanger grates use a fan to draw in cool room air, reheat it in the grate tubing, and force it back into the room. An air supply at the base of one type of grate increases fire temperature to burn off pollutants.

A kiva is the classic Southwestern version of a corner fireplace; it takes up little space yet makes a big architectural statement.

If a fireplace just can't be improved, or if you want a better heat source, consider installing an EPA-approved insert (see page 16). Your challenge is to create a unified look that integrates the insert face with the fireplace surround, mantel, and hearth.

If a gas line is available, installing a ceramic gas log set is an option. Gas logs can be expensive and may require special insulation, but the latest technology has made them an attractive and practical choice for use in wood-burning fireplaces in good condition. For more details, see pages 104–105.

Planning a new installation

Installing an entirely new fireplace in a new or extensively remodeled home calls for serious thought as to design and location. Many of your decisions will be ruled by practical considerations such as foundations (for masonry construction), chimney or vent placement, a fuel source (in the case of gas), and local building codes. Your first step will be to consult with your architect and general contractor, and especially with your fireplace contractor.

Masonry fireplaces and European masonry heaters are the most limited in placement possibilities, since masonry fireplaces require a chimney that vents above the roof level and both types need substantial foundations. Prefab fireplaces and freestanding stoves usually require some kind of venting, through a wall or the roof, but their lighter weight makes placement more flexible. Avoid having an open fireplace near a forced-air furnace outlet register or opposite an outside door; competing drafts may cause downdrafts in the fireplace and chimney.

The size of your firebox, insert, or stove must be appropriate for the space to be heated. Fires should be large enough to provide heat and make an attractive appearance but not so hot as to turn the room into an oven. A fireplace expert can advise you.

Keep in mind the room's traffic patterns as well as doors and windows; you don't want to put the fireplace in the path of traffic. Sometimes a fireplace flanked by large windows—especially if they offer a fine view—is a good solution.

The traditional single-face, flush fireplace has the firebox facing the room on the same plane as the wall (or recessed and flanked by shelving or cabinetry). Other possible configurations include multiface fireplaces that are L-shaped or three-faced, to be viewed from several angles. A see-through fireplace can act as a room divider and give you double pleasure from your fire. A corner fireplace can be tucked into a small space to charming effect.

You can opt for an arched fireplace opening rather than a square one, or for a firebox above floor level so that a raised hearth acts as a footrest or a seat. Some manufactured fireplaces can be placed quite high on the wall, making them good options for bathrooms, bedrooms, or small rooms with no space for a hearth.

Talk to your fireplace dealer and contractor about what options might fit into your project. Don't forget to take chimney and venting requirements into account.

Gas logs and a set of handsome nickel-plated brass andirons (above left) are a perfect marriage of beauty and practicality. Below, prefab fireplace technology is the secret of this see-through fireplace—centerpiece of a room divider that defines distinct areas in a light-filled open space.

fireplace face-lifts

AESTHETICS may be the major motivator for making improvements to an existing fireplace that is in good working order. If that's the case, you can concentrate on the decorative elements—facings, mantel, and hearth—to turn an outdated or unattractive fireplace into a visual asset.

It was so simple—painting the old brick a crisp white conferred instant star status on this intriguing fireplace and exposed chimney.

Quick fireplace fixes

If you're generally happy with the style and materials of your fireplace, sometimes just a little cleaning or painting can make a big difference. These are some quick fixes that are perfectly appropriate as do-it-yourself projects:

- Clean an old stone or brick surround and hearth, repair the mortar, or go a step further and paint it—in fresh white, for example.

- If brick is unsightly, cover it with ceramic or stone tile, available in a wide array of textures and patterns from gleaming marble to rough-textured clay, from elegant Arts-and-Crafts motifs to cheery blue-and-white Delft designs. Or use facing brick, stone, or cultured stone.

- Strip and sand a tired-looking wood mantel to expose the original wood. Apply a stain or simply a fresh coat of paint to cover unattractive wood. Or use faux-painting techniques to achieve an antique or distressed appearance, or even to imitate marble or plaster. Look in craft stores and home centers for kits designed to create these looks.

Remodeling your fireplace

If you're up for a little more serious remodeling, you can completely transform an unattractive fireplace into an eye-catching focal point. Consider what style, color, materials, and ornamentation you want to set the tone of a room or to harmonize with the existing decor. Unless you're a skilled and experienced builder and designer, it's best to consult a professional. You'll also want to double-check local building codes, as they will govern placement of and clearances around the fireplace mantel, surround, and hearth.

You can buy ready-made mantels of wood, cast concrete, or other materials that will work with your existing surround, or have a new mantel and/or surround custom-built (see pages 110–113). Another alternative is an antique mantel and surround; a bit of luck is involved here,

A new concrete mantel and surround with tile accents is the focal point of the comfortable room above. Other remodeling options might include refinishing an original wood mantel (top left) or installing an antique Carrara marble mantel (bottom left).

Wood mantel, paneling, and cabinetry make an elegantly integrated design statement (below). At right, ceramic tile and white-painted wood exude charm. On the facing page, a raised hearth, warm color, and well-orchestrated lighting draw the eye to the fireplace.

since you'll need to get everything to fit your existing fireplace opening. Perhaps your hearth needs revamping; you may want to pour a new one of decorative cast concrete, or lay a seamless stone slab or stone tiles with thin-set mortar. Be sure that your mantel, surround, and hearth are harmonious with one another.

If your remodel includes replacing the firebox—with an insert, for example—the new appliance will usually come with its own trim kit. Some appliances also have an optional surround/mantel/hearth package.

A remodel gives you the freedom to consider broad possibilities such as installing cabinetry or shelving around your fireplace. Built-in book-

shelves flanking the fireplace—or window seats
or media cabinets—can add usable storage and
display space as well as make the fireplace feel
fully integrated into a room. (A mantel can
bridge surrounding shelving or cabinets.)

Other large-scale projects may involve
exposing a brick or stone chimney to make it
an important architectural element, or even
removing walls on either side of the fireplace.
The fireplace then becomes a room divider
that completely changes the flow of a house.
A see-through fireplace that acts as a room
divider is especially dramatic.

Finally, lighting above and around the
fireplace can add drama and warmth. A pair
of matched sconce lights above the mantel is
classic; spotlights on the ceiling, trained on
the front of the fireplace, can add pizzazz. Or
go even further and install recessed lighting in
a soffit over the fireplace for soft highlighting.

CLEAN AIR ISSUES

Gathering around the fireplace is a time-honored pleasure, but in recent times it's not without controversy.
Research has shown that most traditional wood-burning fireplaces—and older wood stoves—are serious polluters of the
air, outdoors and in.

In the 1980s, the Environmental Protection Agency began
developing pollution standards for new wood and coal
stoves and wood-burning prefab fireplaces and inserts, call-
ing for them to burn cleanly at all settings from low to high.
New technology in the form of catalytic combustors, noncatalytic (high-tech) burners, and pellet-fueled stoves has made
this possible (see page 19).

When you buy a new wood-burning stove, prefab fireplace, or insert, look for the label indicating EPA certifica-
tion. An added advantage is increased efficiency: whereas
a traditional masonry fireplace averages less than 15% heating efficiency, a certified stove, insert, or fireplace is 60%
to 80% efficient. Even cleaner and more efficient are gas

burners, and electric heating appliances are 100% efficient
and nonpolluting.

What the EPA doesn't regulate are older fireplaces and
stoves. But you'll want to look for ways to improve even
an allowable "grandfathered" old fireplace—or replace an
inefficient wood stove. You can rebuild a fireplace's firebox
in a Rumford configuration (see page 14), burn only seasoned wood or manufactured logs (using proper fire-
building techniques), and be sure to carefully maintain your
fireplace and chimney.

In many communities, local ordinances take up where
EPA regulations end. Some actually outlaw new construction
of traditional wood-burning fireplaces, in which case an
EPA-approved prefab fireplace or stove is your only wood-
burning alternative. Learn all you can about regulations in
your area before making any choices. Visiting a local fireplace and stove retailer or manufacturer's outlet to talk to
salespeople is one of the best ways to find out what's what.

the hospitable hearth

WHEN YOU DEVOTE *time and energy—and money—to creating a beautiful fireplace, it's probably because you want it to be an important focal point in your home. You can give your fireplace star status through your choice of color and materials, furniture selection and arrangement, and finishing touches such as lighting and accessories.*

The extended hearth of this prefab gas fireplace doubles as a seat; its line is echoed in the mantel and also the beam high above. Bright surrounding walls are a dramatic contrast to the white fireplace.

Focusing on focal points

Any room might have a single natural focal point or several, depending on the size and shape of the space and the positions of key elements. A fireplace is a natural focal point, but so is a large window or a glass patio door—or a big piece of furniture, an important painting or sculpture, or even an impressive houseplant. And, of course,

there's that most compelling of focal points, the television set.

As you evaluate your room, take note of possible focal points, permanent or movable. In anything but a very large or open-plan great room, one or two will be enough. Your challenge is to make your focal points—including the fireplace—work together instead of vying for attention.

A fireplace can work in tandem with another architectural focal point. Flanked by windows or patio doors, it can share light and views in a dynamic way that changes as day turns to night—and the view helps draw attention to the fireplace. Built-in cabinetry or shelving on either side makes a fireplace the center of an entire wall that functions as a focal point. Even a television cabinet (with or without doors) can share the scene with the firebox, giving two viewing options within an integrated scheme.

Some fireplaces are naturally dramatic focal points; a large stone fireplace in a lodge-style room, for example, is already the main attraction. But a more "ordinary" fireplace may need a little help to grab center stage. Here are some ways you can dramatize your fireplace:

- Make it "pop" with contrasting color—paint the fireplace bright white, the adjacent walls a deep color, for example. Alternatively, a dark-hued mantel and surround will stand out against light-colored walls.

- Create eye-catching pattern and color with a tile surround and hearth, or fashion a surround from copper or stainless steel for exciting shimmer.

- Hang a beautiful painting, a mirror, or a striking objet d'art above your fireplace.

- Combine two focal points by hanging an important painting or photograph over the fireplace and spotlighting both art and fireplace with dramatic lighting, or by placing a standing sculpture or large pottery piece to one side of the hearth.

- Use built-in seating—be it a traditional inglenook with seats perpendicular to the fire, built-in benches alongside the fireplace, or a wide ledge that's a continuation of the hearth—to draw the eye while beckoning the viewer to interaction with the fire.

When your fireplace is the focus of the room, its style sets the tone for the whole space. From the rustic style set by a rough stone fireplace to the gleaming formality of a carved-mahogany mantel, the fireplace "calls the shots" when it comes to decorating.

A comfy seating arrangement allows everyone access to two focal points—fireplace and television—that coexist neatly within a well-integrated wall of built-ins.

ONE ROOM, THREE PLANS

Three seating options show how you can focus on the fireplace yet leave room for people to relax and move around in comfort. All provide easy entry into the "inner room."

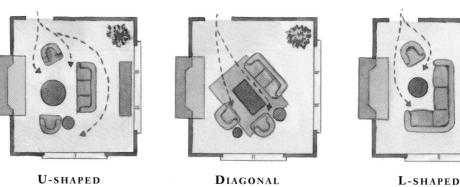

U-SHAPED   **DIAGONAL**   **L-SHAPED**

Creating an inner room

In a thoroughly contemporary setting, a prefab wood-burning fireplace with gas starter shares focal-point status with dramatic windows of glass block and clear glass. All these elements are beautifully spare in design, creating a harmonious, uncluttered arrangement.

In a small room, the fireplace is usually the magnet that attracts everyone; all you need do to create an intimate, welcoming fireside is to position your furniture appropriately. In a large or long room, imagine that you're creating a special "inner room" connected to the rest of the space but slightly separate and more intimate in feeling. You can define this inner room with an area rug and let the backs of sofas and other seating form its boundaries.

The most common furniture arrangement extends out at a right angle from the fireplace, but you can experiment—perhaps angling a rug on a diagonal in front of the fireplace with a sofa or other large piece positioned at a corresponding angle. This can work in either a large or a small room, helping to break up a boxy space.

You don't want any furniture arrangement to block people out; leave an obvious point of entry between pieces of furniture. Often an angled arrangement accomplishes this. A space of 30 to 36 inches between major furnishings allows easiest passage; leave 18 inches between a coffee table and sofa or between chairs. Have at least one chair or sofa facing the entry point; this will clearly say "welcome!"

So that people can view the fire *and* feel comfortable conversing, use a circular, elliptical, or U-shaped arrangement. Try to have a central space about 8 to 10 feet across; this lets people sit across from each other (most people prefer that to side-by-side seating), in an atmosphere that's intimate without feeling crowded. A classic symmetrical arrangement features two chairs flanking the fireplace, a coffee table in the center, and a sofa facing the fire. Or you can place an assortment of chairs in a semicircle around the table.

Another easy arrangement positions two sofas or loveseats perpendicular to the fireplace, facing each other across a coffee table—mimicking the cozy configuration of a built-in inglenook and creating an inner room you can enter but not walk through. Two sofas or loveseats in an L configuration, with one or two chairs opposite, is another workable option.

Many arrangements function best with a generously scaled square coffee table rather than a narrow rectangular one. Or you could opt for a large ottoman; it can be used as fireside seating or, with a tray, as a coffee table. Place small tables near other seating to receive drinks, books, and the like.

Besides your anchor pieces—sofas and large armchairs—you will want versatile furniture to achieve the most flexibility in your fireplace grouping. Consider these possibilities:

- Comfy upholstered swivel chairs let you spin around to face the fire, a television, or the person you're talking to.

- Small, lightweight chairs, upholstered or wooden, can easily be moved into or out of the fireside area as needed.

- Modular furniture pieces can be moved around, pushed together, or pulled apart.

- Small, portable tables can migrate among seating pieces to accommodate drinks, books, and games.

- Ottomans have multiple uses as seats, footrests, tables (with the addition of a tray on top), and sometimes even hidden storage.

- Large floor pillows let you sprawl in front of the hearth or cozy up to the coffee table with your knees tucked under it.

Use color to pull together your inner fireside room. A common upholstery color can unify different furniture and accessory styles. Add a little punch with bright accents positioned

around the space (throws, pillows, and artworks or pottery).

Create a feeling of intimacy at night with lighting. Lamps on tables within the space and around its perimeter create pools of warm light that complement the soft flicker of the fire. (To keep light balanced, try placing lamps in a broad triangle.) Track fixtures above the fireplace area can be angled to focus light wherever you want it. Candles on the mantel and coffee table instantly create a magical atmosphere.

This arrangement could not be more welcoming. A handsome rug defines the fireside area, while a clear point of entry introduces visitors to the bright, open room in which fireplace and windows dominate.

fireplace finery

WHEN THE FOCUS *is on your fireplace, you want it dressed up and looking its best. Your mantel is the perfect place for special treasures—collections, beloved photos, or an impromptu assortment of anything from candles to seashells. Don't forget to pay attention to the wall above and around the fireplace—the ideal canvas for painting a beautiful fireside picture.*

What's your style?

Spare or cheerfully cluttered, casual or formal—what style speaks to you? Certain styles—Victorian, for example, or traditional country—encourage lively, cluttered displays of many small objects. Contemporary style and some classic styles tend in the opposite direction, displaying a few important objects in an uncluttered setting. With "casual" style, almost anything goes—vintage objects mixed with new, shiny with matte, natural with man-made.

Any of these approaches can work on and around your mantel. Following some basic design principles can be your key to success.

A pleasing asymmetrical mantel arrangement balances objects of varying shapes, heights, and materials with an artful eye, creating variety without clutter.

Making arrangements

Begin by clearing your mantel—and the walls around it—of absolutely everything. Then you can try things out, adding and subtracting until your "mantelscape" has the look you're after. Think about three concepts: scale and proportion, unity, and placement.

SCALE AND PROPORTION. These are relatively simple matters when it comes to fireplace decor. A painting over a mantel should not be so big that it overwhelms, nor so small that it's lost. Small artworks are best grouped for greater visual impact. The same goes for objects on the mantel: display small objects in clusters so they catch the eye as a grouping.

Place moderately tall objects on the mantel to visually heighten a small or too-short fireplace; use shorter objects with horizontal lines to give the illusion of greater width. Photos or artwork on either side of the mantel can help "widen" a small fireplace. A mirror over the fireplace is a time-honored way to give the illusion of more space.

UNITY. Achieve unity by selecting display objects according to theme (such as folk art figures), color, or materials and textures (all silver, for instance). If your style is fairly formal, or spare and contemporary, pick fewer objects— ones dramatic enough to stand alone or in a pair.

PLACEMENT. With artful placement, the principles of symmetry and asymmetry, rhythm and variety come into play. Often associated with formal style, symmetry pairs objects that match and balance one another—like identical vases on either side of a painting. Asymmetrical arrangements can create balance and harmony without the precision of symmetry; for example, a large painting placed off-center on the mantel might be balanced with a tall candlestick and a scattering of squat bowls.

To achieve visual rhythm, mix objects that are short and tall, round and angular. For height contrast, set small objects atop decorative boxes or stacked books. Layer things for interest— small objects in front of a picture, for example.

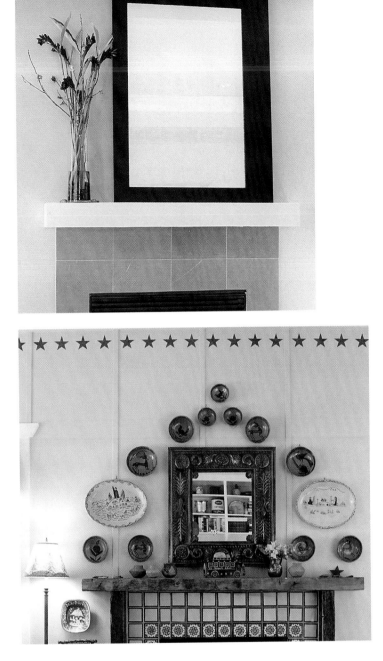

On the walls

When you hang paintings and photographs over and around your fireplace, you may choose to focus attention on one important piece or to create a gallery of smaller works. For a mini-gallery, cut out paper "stand-ins" of proposed pieces and experiment to find the most pleasing arrangement. Keep in mind what you want to display on the mantel, and take into account wall-mounted light fixtures.

A popular casual approach is to prop paintings, photos, and mirrors on the mantel so they're leaning against the wall rather than hanging on it. Just be sure they're firmly anchored.

Utter simplicity is often the most dramatic; at top, a tall mirror balances a vase of flowers in an asymmetrical design. Above, radial symmetry places objects around a central point in a roughly circular pattern.

outdoor
pleasures

ON A COOL SUMMER EVENING *or a crisp autumn afternoon, what could be lovelier than being out-doors on a patio or deck, snuggled up to a glowing fire? It's easy to make this scenario your own. You have a choice between two main approaches: a permanent structure such as a masonry fireplace or fire pit, or a more low-commitment portable fire pit or chiminea.*

Masonry fireplaces

A traditional wood-burning masonry fireplace in your backyard can become the focal point of a fabulous outdoor "room"—a gathering place where family and friends can eat, drink, and be merry. The stone, brick, stucco, or concrete of which fireplaces are built fits into most land-scapes. You can add to the comfort of your out-door fireplace with built-in seating—perhaps as an extension of a raised hearth—or purchased patio furniture. Add to its usefulness by fitting it with a barbecue grill.

The necessary footings, firebrick-lined firebox, and chimney can make a masonry fireplace expensive. One less costly alternative is the out-door version of a fireplace made of lightweight volcanic stone modules. (The indoor model is described on page 15.) You can have one installed on your patio, then clad in stone, tile, or stucco.

Be sure your fireplace won't be too close to your neighbors' house, and take care that smoke will be directed away from their property as much as possible. Don't build the fireplace under low-hanging trees, and equip the chimney with a spark arrester.

If you have space up against the house wall, you may be able to install back-to-back outdoor and indoor fireplaces that share a chimney. Building codes will require the outdoor fireplace to have its own flue.

Fire pits

A low structure built of brick, stone, or concrete in a round or square configuration, a fire pit con-veys the feeling of a campfire. Like a masonry

This gas-fueled fire pit features slate cladding and an elegant metal sculpture that also serves as a wind screen.

fireplace, a fire pit is usually built on-site.

Some fire pits are made to burn wood; others are gas-fired, featuring ceramic "logs" or glowing "coals." A fire pit can easily be made to accommodate a barbecue grill, and it's the perfect place to roast marshmallows!

Prefab fireplaces

Outdoors as well as indoors, you can opt for a lightweight prefab gas-fired or wood-burning fireplace instead of a masonry one. A prefabricated stainless steel shell contains the firebox, and the chimney is metal. Some gas models are front-vented; exhaust is released through slots in the decorative face frame, so you don't even need a chimney.

Like their indoor counterparts, these are zero-clearance units—they can be framed with wood or metal studs, encased in plywood, and finished with stucco, stone, or tile.

Portable choices

If a masonry fireplace or fire pit is too expensive or more permanent than you want, there are less costly, more flexible options.

A *freestanding fire pit* of metal (usually high-carbon steel) may burn wood, propane gas from a hidden tank, or gel alcohol. Round, square, or even teepee-shaped, most have a surround of metal mesh to keep sparks from flying out, with doors you can open.

A popular and inexpensive option is the *chiminea*, a three-legged clay pot modeled on old Mexican bread ovens—though most are meant

for fire-watching only, not for cooking. Chimineas are easy to shift around the patio and simple to use, especially with miniature manufactured logs made specially for them. Some can be used with gas log sets. You'll need a spark screen for a wood-burning chiminea, and a heatproof mat if you're using it on a deck. For a chiminea being used on a porch or in a breezeway, add an extended chimney pipe to vent through the roof.

For more details on portable possibilities, see pages 122–123.

An imposing sculptural chimney and wide raised hearth of concrete make for a dramatic patio fireplace scene.

A GALLERY OF IDEAS

PICTURING YOUR DREAM FIREPLACE is just the turn of a page away—because in this section you'll find a veritable gallery of handsome fireplaces, one of which is sure to help you envision your own. We've searched out fireplaces and stoves of all descriptions, from contemporary creations of steel or glass to comfortable classics of rough fieldstone or hand-rubbed wood. **THE TECHNOLOGIES** that make them all work are as varied as their outward appearances, and often the "nuts and bolts" aren't even visible. Rest assured that you can marry practically any technology to any decorative style. **GO STYLE SHOPPING** in the following pages, then take the ideas you've collected to your chosen fireplace professionals to turn your dream into a reality.

classic fireplaces

IN MANY PEOPLE'S EYES, the charms of the fireside call forth visions of an era when life was lived at a slower, easier pace and daily activities were centered on home and family. Perhaps that's why many of us gravitate to fireplace styles that evoke the past. In the following pages, you'll see a tantalizing sampling of classic styles, some with pure vintage charm, some with the flavor of a particular locale and era, and some that employ new materials to interpret traditional designs or to give them a subtly updated look.

Even as we celebrate classic styles, we appreciate new technologies that allow us to have our cake and eat it, too. We can enjoy the old-fashioned charms of the fireplace along with the cleanliness and efficiency of

prefabricated fireplaces, the warmth afforded by fireplace inserts, the convenience of gas-fired fireplaces. Among the photos on these pages, you'll see examples of some of these "new" fireplaces, masterfully integrated into traditional settings.

As you contemplate the fireplaces in the following pages, notice how the rooms in which they are found reflect and enhance their styles. Wall treatments, surrounding cabinetry and windows, furnishings, and art all contribute to a warm, welcoming, and gracious traditional ambience. These are true classics!

Set into a turret wall, the fireplace at left is an original part of a 1920s home in the Italian country style. The old brick was faux-painted a soft apricot; persimmon accents bring the niche, fireplace opening, and hearth into focus. The fire screen is a French antique. A European pottery piece (right) makes a unique log holder that carries out the Italian country theme.

The simple lines of the white plaster
mantel and surround above
showcase a one-of-a-kind fire screen
crafted of wrought iron in a
handsome leaf design. Behind the
screen is an efficient prefab
gas fireplace.

In a fresh interpretation of a classic look, the simple painted wood mantel for this flush-mounted fireplace was designed to continue the room's deep baseboards. Within a one-of-a-kind surround of spectacular art tiles is a custom-made fire curtain.

For a new Craftsman home built on a grand scale (left), an important fireplace was a must. The cherry-stained alder mantel and hearth platform match woodwork throughout the house. The ceramic tiles (both the "relief" art tiles and the plainer "field" tiles) were custom-made. Tucked into this classic setting is a contemporary wood-burning prefab firebox.

In a gracious 1910 Craftsman home, the original fireplace had a failing masonry firebox surrounded by broken ceramic tiles. The architect owner had the firebox rebuilt and replaced the tiles with custom-colored ones. The Douglas fir mantel and woodwork were stripped of darkened shellac and given a new, lightened lease on life. To add style and solve the problem of a poorly drawing fireplace, the owner designed a hand-hammered copper piece to reduce the size of the firebox opening.

A snug dining area off the family kitchen centers on this charming cottage-style fireplace. A wood mantel featuring classic moldings painted white pairs nicely with a rustic stone surround. Above the fireplace, an artfully placed selection of mirrors is a simple but delightful decorating idea.

Executed in wood with graceful curves and fresh white paint, this mantel and overmantel with beveled mirror offer plenty of Old World charm. An original design element is the surround of old-style pressed tin ceiling tiles. A modern gas prefab fireplace provides warmth and dancing flames.

The harmonious space at left was the result of a major remodel that included bumping out the wall to accommodate a new wood-burning prefab fireplace. A pair of windows was added above custom-built cabinets, one of which holds a TV. The custom mantel is a perfect blend with the original Victorian woodwork, and a fireplace surround of glass mosaic tiles creates a fresh look.

This fireplace was fashioned to harmonize with the house's gracefully aged South-of-the-Border style, which makes use of salvaged ceiling beams and floor tiles. The unique mantel and hearth were hand-carved of Mexican Cantera stone. The firebox itself is newly built of masonry in a Rumford configuration; a gas starter makes lighting fires a snap.

"Contemporary country" is the style moniker for this lovely room. A faux chimney of gypsum board textured with plaster helps the fireplace measure up to 13-foot ceilings and custom cabinets. A plain little prefab firebox (wood-burning with gas starter) is dressed up with a custom wrought-iron screen, its frame echoing dentil molding on the cabinets. For the mantel, the designer used faux painting to "age" wood crown molding; metal corbels from an architectural salvage yard provide support.

A state-of-the-art prefab gas fireplace is paired with traditional French country styling to dramatic effect. Flanked by classic diamond-pane casement windows, the plaster mantel, hearth, and exposed faux chimneypiece lend Old World grace to an intimate seating area. Above the curve of the raised hearth, a custom-built screen and ornate andirons carry out the elegant look.

A wood-burning masonry fireplace has been dressed up with a new wood mantel designed to function visually as a single unit with the arched niches on either side. Shelves were added under the niches, and white paint unifies and brightens the entire space.

To achieve the stunning French country look in this luxurious study, custom-built pine woodwork, fireplace mantel, and cabinetry are all of a piece, stained and distressed for a convincingly antique appearance. The gleaming dark marble of the fireplace surround and hearth offers a dramatic contrast to the wood's warmth.

For this cottage on the site
of an old dairy barn,
the architects fantasized
a fireplace reminiscent of
one left standing after the
building around it had
long since crumbled. They
gave this fireplace of local
stone a stepped exposed
chimney and an arched
opening to suggest that
long-ago feeling in a light
and airy new space.

Constructed of Colorado
bluestone, the generously
proportioned fireplace at
left is the focal point of a
cozy but elegant bungalow.
The arched design of the
firebox opening is echoed
in the display niche above.
A pair of small spotlights
was built into the under-
side of the arch to highlight
objects arranged below.

A rustic cottage-style bluestone fireplace surrounds a modern wood-burning prefab firebox in this successful partnership of ambience and practicality. The mantel is made of recycled barn wood; for whimsy, the architect added a "mousehole." A handmade tile set into the stone was a serendipitous find with a hometown theme.

Constructed with painstaking care from dry-stacked square stones, this imposing fireplace features a dramatic arched niche above a massive Douglas fir mantel. The wood-burning classic (with gas starter) calls to mind cozy evenings at a mountain lodge.

It looks like antique stone, but the elegant fireplace below actually has a veneer of crushed limestone applied over a steel frame covered with noncombustible foam. Artful etching mimics blocks of stone; the "carved" relief above the gas firebox is cast of the same stone material. Hand finishing creates a convincing pitted surface and brings out the limestone's patina.

Carved of wood, the ornate period mantel above was faux-finished to match the antique look of custom furnishings in this living room. A dark marble surround frames a traditional wood-burning fireplace updated with a gas starter. At left, a substantial fireplace original to this circa-1906 home was built to last of local stone and charmingly irregular clinker bricks. The handsome redwood and fir woodwork is also original, as are the hammered-bronze and glass light fixtures. The fire screen was custom-made to incorporate antique andirons representing Diana and Apollo.

Above: A light touch was used to dress up this fireplace for the holidays with a swag of seasonal fruits and greens. A simple wreath hung in the place of honor above the mantel provides a charming holiday focal point. Right: To add holiday cheer without lighting a fire, try placing a special fireplace candelabra in your firebox. Add votive candles and dress up the firebox with a few pine cones, and you've created a special kind of fireside warmth.

*An old-fashioned Christmas
looks exactly like this: the
tree, wreath, and fireplace
swag blend perfectly with
the rustic room decor.
When using greens near the
fireplace, be sure they're
fresh, and don't position
them too close to the firebox.*

*Candles in lavish
profusion team up with
simple winter greens and
seasonal fruits to add a
festive touch to a substantial stone fireplace. Using
greenery to frame a picture
or mirror hanging above
a fireplace is a good way
to give it a holiday air.*

state-of-the-art style

Sleek, sophisticated, and innovative, today's cutting-edge fireplace designs bring an element of excitement to contemporary rooms. Pairing new technology with nontraditional design makes sense from both practical and aesthetic standpoints. The spare black or metallic facings of many prefabricated fireboxes blend well with the clean lines, sleek materials, and bold colors used for fireplace surrounds as well as with other decorative elements executed in the modern design idiom. And prefabs allow for fireplace installation in configurations that have a contemporary feel—as room dividers, for example, or between large windows.

Materials favored for contemporary design—smooth and shiny stainless steel, versatile concrete, recycled glass, cast stone—give today's fireplaces a distinctively different look from their traditional forebears. Such materials also make nontraditional shapes possible.

Minimalist style inspires new takes on mantels, too. Some designs dispense with them completely, while others make use of unusual materials to create spare, geometrical mantels. Hearths may be simple platforms of stone or concrete, or raised ledges. Some prefab gas and electric fireplaces don't require any hearth at all—a gleaming floor surface of tile or even wood meets the fireplace in an unbroken expanse.

However it's interpreted, the "new" fireplace has been transformed by innovative design into a focal point that's dramatic, playful, or even startling—but always interesting.

This tiny prefab gas fireplace is perfect for a small space or an area where mantel-and-hearth construction isn't necessary or wanted.

The owner of the bright urban home at right wanted a fireplace but didn't want to block the natural light or the view with a bulky chimney. The solution: a prefab gas fireplace that could be vented directly out the back. With its sleek marble-faced surround, the fireplace functions as a key architectural element and serves as a practical source of heat for the open-plan room.

This spectacular glass fireplace is acid-etched on the surface and mirrored in back for sheen and brilliance. When it's too warm for a fire, exuberant sprays of forsythia maintain the fireplace's star status.

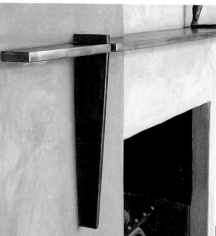

In a handsome modernist house, back-to-back fireplaces (shown below and on the facing page) shared a brick chimney that formed the central core for an open-plan living area. In the process of remodeling, the masonry fireboxes were retained but the brick was sheathed in gypsum board. Below, colored plaster defines interlocking gypsum board shapes on one side. The asymmetrical steel mantel has an elegant sculptural quality.

The reverse side of the fireplace on the facing page
is this L-shaped version
framed with a spare,
bold surround of steel.
Its simplicity acts as a
perfect foil for pieces from
the owners' fine modern
art collection.

A state-of-the-art,
see-through gas prefab
fireplace does duty for
two adjoining spaces—the
living and dining areas.
The handsome and cleverly
designed room divider
includes plenty of storage
space; in addition, it
offers display shelving
all around as well as
a raised hearth for
additional seating.

Set into a dramatically curved wall painted intense Prussian blue, this may be the ultimate in modernistic bedroom fireplaces. The prefab gas firebox, which can be operated from the bed by a remote control, is actually back-to-back with another fireplace on the concave side of the wall.

With fireplace mantel and walls done in taupe plaster, this serene living room (left) presents a pleasingly unified picture. The fireplace is site-built masonry, wood-burning with a gas starter. Above the mantel is the perfect place to display an original work by the owner/artist.

The bold geometry of this fireplace design was executed in gypsum board painted the color of the grasses that grow just outside the windows. A paint additive gives the wall a stucco-like texture; the facing of the firebox (a wood-burning prefab) is a sleek contrast in black steel. The cast-in-place concrete hearth doubles as a bench.

Innovative is the word for both the styling and the choice of materials in this living-room fireplace. A steel I-beam mantel caps a surround of concrete densely embedded with fragments from recycled yellow traffic lights, giving it a terrazzo-like look (see detail at right). The firebox is a gas prefab with fixed-glass front. Lights above the fireplace spotlight the artwork over the mantel.

This installation has an air of rustic coziness, but the technology and design treatment are distinctly contemporary. The gas fireplace features preset temperature control and remote-control operation. A dramatic surround of slate tiles is topped with an eye-catching cedar beam. The raised position is both dramatic and practical: heat gets distributed widely, and the flames can be seen from almost anywhere.

The focus for family room gatherings, a prefab gas fireplace gets a touch of elegance from a surround of gleaming cast stone. The clean, spare lines of this fireplace, raised and flush-mounted into the wall, give it a contemporary look and make it easy to fit into a small space.

An L-shaped fireplace, positioned above a raised hearth and open to view from several angles, draws the spaces of an open-plan house together. The hearth is of cast concrete embedded with rocks picked out by the designer's daughter; the fireplace wall is integrally colored plaster. The designer left the metal chimney exposed to function as a design element in itself. For another view, see page 67.

The fireplace at right is modern in spirit yet pays homage to the work of past California architects such as Maybeck and Morgan. Board-formed cast-in-place concrete created a distinctive surface texture; the precast mantel displays ceramics made by the owner's daughter. The custom-colored concrete floor eliminates the need for a noncombustible hearth.

LIGHTING IT RIGHT

Laying a good fire takes practice, but once you get the knack of it you'll be able to lay a fire that starts quickly, burns evenly, and produces plenty of heat. Such a fire actually burns more cleanly than a sluggish, poorly maintained one.

Begin by putting several crumpled or twisted sheets of newspaper on your grate or (for a wood stove or insert) firebox floor. Then create a structure of kindling (small, thin sticks of fast-burning softwood) by laying several pieces in crisscross fashion on top of the paper. Now place three fairly small, fully seasoned logs on the kindling, split sides down, one on top of the other two (see the drawing at right). This will confine the fire's heat to the center, with each log radiating heat to the other two. Be sure not to stack the logs so tightly that the fire can't escape upward and burn evenly.

Check to make sure the damper is open in your fireplace, insert, or stove. If you feel a cold downdraft, create an upward draft in a fireplace chimney by making a twist of newspaper, lighting it, and holding it high in the throat of the fireplace so that the smoke rises; then use it to light the paper underneath the kindling. For a wood stove or insert, place a balled-up piece of newspaper as high up toward the chimney as you can and carefully light it; it should immediately get sucked upward. Light the paper under the kindling before the draft can reverse itself.

If you have a wood stove or insert, close its door as soon as you've lit the newspaper; the stove's regulated draft should get the fire off to a good start. With a fireplace, close the glass doors as soon as the newspaper catches fire in order to increase the draft and keep smoke out of the room. (Open them once the fire's going, to avoid excess heat buildup—see page 117.) If there are no doors, put the fire screen in place unless you'll be watching the fire closely.

LOGS

KINDLING

CRUMPLED
NEWSPAPER

heart of the home

NOTHING SAYS "HOME" like a fireplace right in your kitchen or dining room. Though not the necessity for cooking that it was in days past, a fireplace can provide an inviting focal point in everybody's favorite part of the house.

Traditionally, kitchen and dining room fireplaces have been built flush with the wall, with hearths at floor level or slightly elevated. But today's models offer additional configurations, such as fireplaces built higher into the wall so that diners and cooks have a full view of the fire and feel more of its warmth. A corner fireplace is particularly well suited to a small kitchen or dining area, be it the distinctive kiva style of the American Southwest or an updated version.

Though many kitchen fireplaces are strictly for show rather than for food preparation, others offer the opportunity for some serious cooking. You can outfit yours with a built-in grill or purchase a separate Tuscan-style grill to slide in when the occasion calls for fireplace cookery. Another possibility is a built-in wood-burning pizza or bread oven, a tradition borrowed from Europe.

Some of the fireplaces on the following pages, like gas-fired prefabricated models, are fairly simple to add to a kitchen or dining room. Others—a masonry pizza oven, for example—may have to be planned along with the construction of the room. Explore the possibilities in detail by talking to a fireplace dealer, architect, kitchen designer, or fireplace contractor.

A French-style wood-burning bread oven lends delightful ambience to the cozy breakfast nook pictured at right. The plaster façade has classic European styling; marble is a practical surface for the hearth. The alcoves below the oven are for display and close-at-hand wood storage.

A festive dinner has extra panache when enjoyed by a blazing fire. A corner fireplace like the one at left is often ideal for a dining area because it takes up little room; a raised hearth ensures a good view of the flames.

With a portable Tuscan grill like this, you can turn any fireplace into a mini-kitchen. Meat, poultry, fish, and vegetables cooked on the grill have a delectably charred, wood-smoked flavor. Why not throw a grill-it-yourself party and get your guests into the act?

Like a painting on the wall, a sleek prefab gas fireplace provides an eye-level view for diners. The "frame" is custom-made of copper treated with acid.

Set into a dry-stacked stone façade, the prefab fireplace at right gently warms a dining space and open kitchen as winter light pours through glass-paned French doors.

In a sophisticated version of a cabin kitchen, the L-shaped fireplace at left supplies warmth, a lovely glow, and a cooking fire all at the same time. The copper hood provides ventilation.

In the kitchen/dining area at left, a raised wood-burning fireplace with a built-in spit allows open-fire roasting of meats and poultry. The design incorporates wood storage and a display shelf, creating an interesting focal point of three rectangles in descending sizes.

This contemporary L-shaped fireplace (also pictured on page 60) warms an elliptical dining space defined by the curve of the dark-stained flooring.

A kiva-style fireplace, raised to form a counter-height hearth with wood storage beneath, anchors one side of the Southwest-style kitchen below.

the intimate hearth

To GAZE AT A COZY FIRE as you snuggle down under the bedclothes or recline in the bathtub is surely a dream come true. Fortunately, it's a dream that doesn't have to be out of reach. Because prefabricated fireplaces can be installed in upper stories and retrofitted into rooms that haven't had fireplaces before, bedroom and bathroom fireplaces are becoming more affordable and popular. And many people who remodel or build are opting for the ultimate: a see-through or double-sided fireplace shared by both rooms.

In the days before central heating, homes of a certain stature often had a fireplace in each bedroom. These traditional wood-burning fireplaces are still found in many older homes; if you have one, you can upgrade it or give it a face-lift as described in the previous section of this book, "Planning & Design." An even better option might be to retrofit it as a gas fireplace. This has the advantage of being both clean and easy to manage—you can even "light" many models from bed using a remote control.

As for bathroom fireplaces, in the "good old days" a tub was often set in front of the fire in the family kitchen or a bedroom, then filled with water. Fireplaces in today's bathrooms are a big improvement on that scenario! The bathroom, like the bedroom, is a good candidate for a gas fireplace.

If you want to add a new fireplace to a bedroom or bath in your home, your first steps are to consult a professional and to learn how local building codes govern such installations.

Originally wood-burning, this bedroom fireplace was retrofitted for gas and outfitted with a mural of blue-and-white tiles.

In the remodeled bedroom/sitting room at right, the dividing wall was opened with a graceful arch and a see-through fireplace. In keeping with the elegant decor, the designer chose a French-style mantel of cast stone for the prefab gas fireplace; the raised hearth is a piece of limestone chosen to match.

Sleek and spare, a contemporary bedroom and bathroom suite features gleaming surfaces and a pale, soothing palette. The see-through prefab gas fireplace contributes to the clean-lined, open look and makes bathing in the large tub pure luxury.

Above: Southwestern style looks fresh and up to date in this airy bedroom. The kiva fireplace sets the tone; its elevated firebox allows a view of the fire from the comfort of the bed, and a niche below accommodates wood storage.

Left: In an old-fashioned bedroom, the original fireplace looks great even without a fire; a vintage towel rack holding snowy linens dresses up the empty firebox.

In summer, try an old tradition: display a lovely fire board like this in front of the empty firebox.

Cleverly positioned to mimic the fireside bathing ritual of bygone days, this clawfoot tub has been plumbed in place right in front of the old brick fireplace. White paint, dainty wallpaper, and charming decorative touches add vintage charm.

A display of fine pottery pieces lends distinction to this bathroom fireside scene. The dramatic simplicity of the gas fireplace's surround provides a good foil for the collection; the two-way fireplace also warms the adjacent bedroom.

Bathtub relaxation is enhanced by the dancing flames in a see-through gas prefab fireplace, which can also be enjoyed from the master bedroom, seen below. The bathroom installation dispenses with a hearth to save space; in the bedroom, a raised hearth functions as an impromptu side table for an easy chair.

A luxurious master bedroom like the one at left calls for an intimate conversation space; chairs are drawn up to a lovely fireplace that's the focal point of the room. Behind glass doors, a gas fire adds its glow to the room's soft electric lighting. The raised firebox allows a view of the fire from the bed.

stylish
transformations

As **THE DRAMATIC PICTURES** on the following pages demonstrate, no homeowner has to be stuck with an unattractive or outdated fireplace. The "magic wand" that transforms a fireplace can be as simple as a paintbrush or as complex as an architect's drawing pencil, but something will work in almost any situation.

Some of the remodels you'll see here are large-scale projects in which the fireplace was a part of an entire room redo. With such a project, you can (depending on your budget) add or subtract windows, resurface walls, add new built-ins and lighting, and remodel the fireplace itself. On a smaller scale, you might just reface the existing fireplace, add a new mantel or hearth, and paint or wallpaper the surrounding wall.

When working with the fireplace surround and mantel, make sure you know the specifics of local building codes governing how far combustible materials must be from the firebox. When it comes to choosing materials and techniques for refacing your fireplace, a designer, architect, contractor, or other professional can advise you about the almost dazzling range of options, from stainless steel tile to special adhesives and wall finishes. If you aren't working with a professional, talk to knowledgeable salespeople at a local fireplace dealer, home center, or large hardware store.

At left, the redo of a ho-hum prefab firebox in a loft apartment combines countrified whimsy with industrial pizzazz. The wall was given a heavy plaster coat for strength and texture. The wood mantel, "aged" with faux painting, is supported by custom-designed steel legs. The substantial fire screen effectively covers up the firebox. The floor is concrete, so no outer hearth was needed. An original Picasso print confers star status.

BEFORE

AFTER

With its substantial hearth, the original brick fireplace was just too big for this California bungalow. In remodeling, the owner/designer kept the wood-burning masonry firebox, situated between two windows, and part of the brick face. The face was plastered over and the opening redone as a graceful curve without a hearth. Then the wall was given a warm Provençal glow with plaster integrally tinted by French earth pigments.

AFTER

BEFORE

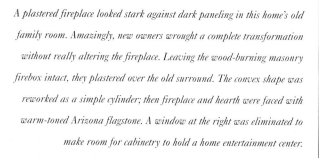

A *plastered fireplace looked stark against dark paneling in this home's old family room. Amazingly, new owners wrought a complete transformation without really altering the fireplace. Leaving the wood-burning masonry firebox intact, they plastered over the old surround. The convex shape was reworked as a simple cylinder; then fireplace and hearth were faced with warm-toned Arizona flagstone. A window at the right was eliminated to make room for cabinetry to hold a home entertainment center.*

Originally, the owner/designer installed a wood stove rather than build the costly two-story masonry chimney required for a fireplace in this room with vaulted ceiling. Then the advent of the zero-clearance prefab wood-burning fireplace made it possible to use a simple metal chimney, vented out the back. A marble tile surround and a ready-made mantel, customized and painted, complete the picture.

AFTER

BEFORE

BEFORE

AFTER

When making over a cramped living room into a soaring two-story parlor, the architect transformed the original painted-brick fireplace with sculpturally ribbed cast concrete and a surround of gleaming stainless steel tiles. A large mantel mirror adds drama and light.

A nondescript 50-year-old fireplace needed updating, though the masonry firebox was fine. The owner installed a new surround and hearth of slate tiles, then created a new face of drywall covered with noncombustible clay plaster in sand color. The new mantel is black walnut.

BEFORE

AFTER

AFTER

BEFORE

Redoing this fireplace was part of a comprehensive remodel of a 1950s home. Slate tiles replaced the brick fireplace surround, freshening its contemporary simplicity. Warm color, a dramatic painting, display niches on each side, and artful lighting combine to make a harmonious picture.

warming stoves

WHEN YOU WANT reliably toasty warmth, a freestanding stove fills the bill. A stove packs a lot of heat-giving properties into a small package thanks to its efficient operation, which circulates as well as radiates heat, and its freestanding position, which allows more heat to radiate throughout a room. (Its close cousin, the fireplace insert, has similar heat-giving properties, though it projects from a fireplace opening rather than being freestanding.) Whether fired by wood, pellets, gas, coal, or even electricity, a stove can warm a large or small room, depending on its size.

With today's styling, a freestanding stove can lend your home a look that's casual and cabin-cozy or sleek and contemporary. Wood stoves have long been traditional in mountain and ski cabins, providing welcome warmth after a day out on the lake or whizzing down the snowy slopes. But now the classic black stove has been joined by gleaming enamel-clad models that can be any color, from sophisticated cream to fire-engine red—with stovepipes to match.

And in place of an unrelieved cast-iron or steel face, most stoves now have generously sized glass doors that let you watch the roaring flames. Even pellet stoves—once plain, square, and uninteresting in appearance—are offered in charming designs and colors.

The last word in sophistication is provided by European freestanding stoves and masonry heaters. Made of steel, ceramic, or soapstone, European-style stoves feature spare, contemporary shapes—usually tall and cylindrical, with built-in wood storage beneath. Large masonry heaters, designed to absorb heat from a hot fire and radiate it for hours through heavy soapstone walls, can be architectural elements in their own right.

Against a practical (and fireproof) tile backdrop, a state-of-the-art European wood stove warms the house and offers a view of flickering flames.

A wood stove is always right at home in a woodsy cabin like the one at right. Here it's in an especially dramatic setting, beneath a rusticated railing of alder saplings that gives the space the look of an indoor forest.

A 1926 coal-burning fireplace originally occupied this space; the owners wisely kept the beautiful tile surround but retrofitted it with a brand-new pellet stove insert. Now the fireplace actually warms the room while retaining its one-of-a-kind vintage looks.

Once homely, pellet stoves have come into their own, design-wise. The handsome example at right, dressed up in sleek black porcelain enamel and chrome, is a copy of a Victorian parlor stove. It's not just for show: this efficient heater can keep a generous space toasty. It sits on stone tiles for safety.

With its heavy soapstone walls and interior, a European masonry heater (left) radiates a gentle heat that can warm a cabin for many hours. The stone here has been built out around ductwork to form a ledge under the windows, adding a handsome architectural element to the room.

A wood stove is right at home in a cozy vintage home—actually a converted 19th-century factory. The native stone walls are a practical backdrop for this wood-burning beauty, which features an extra-wide "window" for viewing the crackling fire.

Tucked snugly into a niche of slate tiles, a good-looking wood stove warms and cheers the family room at left. A clever secret is hidden in a built-in cherry cabinet to the right: the doors open to the house exterior, letting the homeowner reach in to grab firewood from outside.

In a wonderfully light open-plan kitchen-dining-living area, a contemporary European wood stove is the centerpiece of a cleverly designed room divider. The stove's materials and design are reflected in the log storage units on either side, connected by the platform "hearth."

*Brick is a traditional fireplace material,
so it's a natural to use in a niche for a
freestanding stove. The brick does a good
job of absorbing and radiating the fire's
heat, and its warm color is a perfect foil
for this perky red enamel propane model.
The arched niche design lends old-
country ambience.*

*Perched on a platform of river rock, the
wood-burning stove below functions as
the primary source of winter heat for a log
home. Cedar, oak, and fir fuel hot, clean-
burning fires; a cast-iron steamer atop the
stove keeps the air from getting too dry.*

This wood stove's setting is full of history. The rocks were collected over 15 years from the area around the owner's California gold-country home. Besides looking handsome, they help warm the room by absorbing and radiating the stove's heat. Hangers projecting from the stone are 19th-century railroad spikes.

the great outdoors

IT'S LIKE CAMPING OUT in style when you, your family, and friends gather around an outdoor fireplace. Whether yours is a full-fledged fireplace or a modest chiminea, it is certain to be the focal point for many a cozy, convivial gathering. On a chilly weekend afternoon or a mild evening, a fire can be the center around which you enjoy a meal, a chat, or a time of quiet contemplation. As part of a comprehensive patio or deck design, it becomes the heart of an outdoor "room" in which furnishings, plants, water features, and even lighting create a special magic.

On the following pages, you'll see a selection of outdoor fireplace types and styles available nowadays. Site-built fireplaces, the outdoor counterparts of indoor masonry fireplaces, offer all the style options of their indoor cousins—traditional to contemporary, rough-hewn to refined. As with indoor fireplaces, you have a choice of technologies, from wood-burners with gas starters to prefabricated gas-fueled fireplaces. (For more information about outdoor options, see pages 122–123.) You'll also see fireplaces designed for covered areas, as well as one that's set up for grilling.

Less elaborate options include built-in and portable fire pits and sturdy little chimineas. These charming fireplaces are so lightweight that you can move them about on your patio or deck as the mood strikes you.

With its handsome fireplace and flanking storage niches, a covered patio makes a cozy outdoor "room."

Lake Herman bluestone confers rugged outdoor appeal to the patio fireplace and raised hearth at right. The firebox was built from a kit in the heat-efficient Rumford configuration. Shelter in the form of an arbor and an umbrella gives the space an intimate atmosphere.

A portable fire pit is just the ticket when you want a small patio fire without the expense and permanence of a site-built fireplace. This unit uses propane or natural gas.

Set into a dry-stacked stone
wall, this substantial
fireplace and its wide
chimney form a focal point
for outdoor entertaining.
The wood-burning firebox
is built to a Rumford
configuration; the
chimney's wide rain cap
was custom-made.
Flagstone-topped seats on
either side are cozy perches.

In a covered outdoor room
linking two parts of a California
wine-country home, the fireplace
at left was designed for serious
cooking. The owners use a
custom-built adjustable grill
to cook over a wood fire;
a copper hood guides cooking
smoke up the chimney. The
concrete counter-cum-hearth
is a practical work surface.

The graceful curve of a fireplace
forms one side of the pleasant
outdoor "room" pictured above.
Twin niches—the prefab firebox
and a storage area for wood—are
contained in a simple structure of
concrete block sheathed in stucco.
Arizona flagstone on the raised
hearth matches the patio surface.
At left, an idyllic setting calls for
a gracious vantage point—here, a
patio featuring a kiva-style fireplace
beneath a roof of Spanish clay tiles.

*Fashioned of cast concrete in the grand
European country style, this generously
proportioned patio fireplace has a twin
in the sun room just inside.*

*In this minimalist desert garden, a simple fire pit in a
stone bowl adds evening drama to a poolside scene—
a study in cool azure and shades of green.*

Designed to tie in with house architecture and materials, this wood-burning fireplace is built of stone with a distinctive shingled chimney. Stone benches flank the structure, their curved configuration helping to define the patio's rear boundary.

The ultimate in up-to-date convenience, this outdoor fireplace features a prefab firebox and surround with a metal chimney. It's zero-clearance, so it can be fitted into a wood- or metal-stud framework and covered with plywood or backerboard, then finished with stucco.

*With several garden "rooms" for entertaining, the owner envisioned a fireplace evocative of the storybook
cottages of Carmel, California. The result is this charming outdoor fireplace (below and right) accented
with stone and delightfully irregular clinker brick. In the gazebo, handmade willow chairs are pulled up
to the hearth. A log cradle keeps firewood handy, and a built-in gas starter makes lighting fires a snap.*

With the fireplace and its quirky chimney as a quaint backdrop, another seating area is warmed by a simple clay chiminea on a "floor" of stone and gravel. Rustic wooden furniture carries out the storybook style of the garden amid a profusion of flowers and lush shrubbery. The lightweight chiminea can easily be moved as the occasion dictates.

A
SHOPPER'S
GUIDE

Once, having a fireplace in your home meant you had it built—brick by brick or stone by stone—by a mason. You can still do that, but today you also have a wealth of other options, in both the substance and the style of your fireplace or stove. The following pages provide a sampling of what you can find in today's market. On the practical side, you'll see the latest in wood-burning, gas-fired, and electric prefab fireplaces, stoves, inserts, and portable outdoor fireplaces. You'll also learn about your fuel options. Combining the aesthetic with the practical, you'll find a brief survey of the various materials—from polished wood to state-of-the-art cast concrete—that you can choose for your fireplace mantel and surround. Finally, we offer a selection of tools and accessories for any fireplace or stove.

Prefabricated Fireplaces

TODAY'S CHOICES OFFER STYLE AND EFFICIENCY

Whatever terminology you use to describe them—prefab, factory-made, manufactured, or zero-clearance—these modern fireplaces represent the epitome of efficiency and style. Available as units fueled by wood, gas, or electricity, they come in a surprising array of designs, from traditional fireplace faces to sleek contemporary interpretations.

Prefab fireplaces are available in single- and multi-faced as well as see-through versions; there are also outdoor models. The firebox usually has a visible metal faceplate, offered in a variety of designs from Victorian-style cast iron to sleek polished brass, pewter, or nickel.

These fireplaces can be installed with almost any kind of facing, mantel, and hearth—from wood to stone—that you could use with a traditional fireplace. (Many fireplace makers offer ready-made mantels, facings, and cabinets as well as trim kits for a finished installation.) Some can also be placed high on a wall or installed two-sided.

Many prefabs come with glass doors for heat efficiency and fire-viewing, and many manufacturers offer outside air systems that work continuously to keep the glass clean. Many gas prefabs have a fixed glass front rather than a glass door that opens. Optional features include heat-circulating fans and energy-saving dampers.

> ## BEFORE YOU BUY
>
> Look for the EPA certification sticker on any prefab fireplace, insert, or stove you are considering. Have your dealer explain the technology, venting requirements, and other specifics that pertain to particular models that interest you. Ask for help in figuring out what kind of fireplace will work best in the location you have in mind.

Although some factory-built fireplaces allow for "clean-face" installation, most have heat exchanger grilles, or vents, above and below the firebox to allow cold room air to be drawn in, heated, and circulated back out into the room. These grilles may be simple louvers or masked with fancy metalwork.

To shop for a prefab fireplace, visit fireplace dealers and look on the Internet, where you'll find numerous dealers and manufacturers (for a start, see pages 124–125). Consult your professional helpers—building contractor, architect, and chimney sweep—to learn what will work best in your situation.

WOOD-BURNING PRE-FABRICATED FIREPLACE

CLEAN-FACE WOOD-BURNING PREFABRICATED FIREPLACE

Wood-burners

Wood-burning prefab models give you the snap, crackle, and glow of a real wood fire, but with increased efficiency. With an insulated steel firebox and a metal chimney for vertical venting to the outdoors, these fireplaces may employ catalytic or noncatalytic burners (see page 19) for pollution-free operation. The firebox is usually lined with refractory material that mimics masonry firebrick.

The best of these fireplaces are so efficient that some models can be connected to your forced air heating system (though this may not be EPA-approved or allowed in your area).

A prefab may have an open firebox that's almost indistinguishable from that of a traditional masonry fireplace, with a clean-face design that allows fireplace facing to be installed right up to the firebox edge (as shown in the photo above).

Gas-fueled systems

Gas-fueled fireplaces offer energy efficiency and a clean burn, and they make it easy to enjoy a fire—all you have to do is turn them on. You can even do that by using a wall switch or a remote control. Thermostats and programmable controls make it a cinch to adjust the heat, the duration, and even the look of a fire.

Many gas fireplaces are so efficient that they are rated as furnaces and can even be used as a primary home heat source. Some manufacturers offer a duct system that carries heat from the fireplace to other rooms; check to find out if this is allowed where you live.

Most gas fireplaces can use propane; if that's the option available to you, check with your dealer to make sure the fireplace you want will work with propane fuel.

The firebox itself is usually lined with refractory material that's a masonry look-alike. Dancing, random-seeming flames burn gas emitted through tiny holes in natural-looking ceramic "logs" piled picturesquely in a fire grate. Some gas-fired units feature burners that look like glowing coals—a great choice for a Victorian-style home with a fireplace that replicates an old coal-burning hearth.

Many gas fireplaces are direct-vent; they have a sealed combustion chamber. Combustion air is drawn in from outside, and combustion by-products are vented outside through a pipe out the top or the back of the fireplace.

GAS-LOG PREFAB
WITH READY-MADE
SURROUND AND HEARTH

This is the only type approved for use in bedrooms. Other gas prefabs are B-vent: they draw in air from the room and vent out combustion by-products, so they must be vented vertically.

Vent-free gas fireplaces require no chimney or vent at all; an oxygen-depletion sensor switch shuts off the fireplace if oxygen falls below safe levels. Their burners also reduce carbon monoxide during combustion. But some health experts advise against using these fireplaces, especially if the house is particularly airtight or if someone in the household has allergies. Several states do not allow their use at all.

GAS-FIRED PREFAB FIREPLACE

Electric fireplaces

The newest and fastest-growing category of fireplaces, electric prefabs can be installed in an existing masonry fireplace or as an all-new system. And, of course, they require no venting.

Although they don't give you the satisfaction of a real fire, new technology has resulted in randomized filtered lighting that simulates glowing logs and flame patterns far more realistically than past attempts. They do produce real heat (though some operate without heat, strictly for show), and you can install them anywhere there's a 120-volt outlet. Most feature a built-in thermostat. Options may include a fan for heat distribution, an air filtration kit, a heatless setting, and a remote control.

CHIMNEY CHECKLIST

A chimney has the all-important function of letting smoke and other products of combustion flow out of the house. Chimneys built today are required to have a *flue lining* of heat-resistant clay tiles, metal (usually stainless steel), or a cast-in-place product resembling cement. (The latter two are the best choices for upgrading or repairing an existing chimney.) Stainless steel chimneys are used with wood-burning or gas-fired stoves, inserts, and manufactured fireplaces.

Atop the chimney, whether it's masonry or metal, a *chimney cap* keeps out rain, helps prevent downdrafts, and deters nest-builders. A *spark arrester* of metal screening keeps hot cinders from flying up onto the roof or surrounding trees. (Many communities require one; find out what's necessary in your area.)

To improve the performance of an older fireplace with a damper that's loose or missing, a top-sealing damper can be retrofitted to the old masonry chimney top. "Draft increasing" or vacuum chimney caps can help solve draft problems.

TOP-SEALING DAMPER

Maintenance

If you use your wood-burning fireplace regularly, you should have the chimney cleaned yearly by a professional chimney sweep to prevent chimney fires. Wood fires, no matter how expertly laid and well-maintained, do generate creosote and soot, and that soot builds up in the chimney whether it's masonry or metal. Even a gas fire (of the yellow-flame variety) generates chimney deposits that must be cleaned out regularly.

A chimney sweep also checks for water leakage or deteriorated mortar and brick and cleans out any nests made by birds or rodents. To find a reliable professional, contact the Chimney Safety Institute of America (see page 124).

CHIMNEY CAP

"HIGH WIND" VENT TOP

LINER AND CAP FOR GAS FIREPLACE

Fireplace Inserts

MAKING IMPROVEMENTS IN THE FIREPLACE YOU HAVE

A variety of devices can be added to your existing masonry fireplace to make it more efficient. Consult with a fireplace contractor to find out which of the following options may be workable for your situation.

Firebox inserts

Installing a new "stove" in your existing wood-burning masonry fireplace will greatly reduce pollution from burning as well as increase heating efficiency. Firebox inserts can be fueled by wood, pellets, gas, or electricity. (For a description of the technologies used in wood- and pellet-burning inserts, see page 19.)

Usually made from plate steel or cast iron, inserts may fit flush with the firebox opening or project a bit onto the outer hearth. The latter configuration provides some additional radiant heat from top, bottom, and sides.

B-VENT GAS INSERT

Like freestanding stoves, inserts usually have glass doors for fire-watching as well as heating efficiency; nearly all have an outside air system that keeps the glass clean. Many offer porcelain enamel finishes in a range of colors. A trim kit allows you to fit the insert neatly into the firebox space.

Inserts usually have blowers for increased heat circulation. Other practical elements include removable ash pans and levelers for uneven hearths.

A pellet insert can be an excellent choice for a fireplace upgrade. Easy to operate, clean, and heat-efficient, pellet-burners offer an even output of heat, especially with a blower. (A pellet insert is pictured on page 83.)

Provided there's a gas source to hook it up to, a gas insert can be installed in an existing masonry fireplace. In most ways, these units look the same and come with the same options as wood-burning inserts, though they may also have remote controls and wall switches or thermostats. Most gas inserts require venting through a chimney liner, though some that are less heat-efficient don't require the liner—check the manufacturer's requirements.

Electric inserts are easiest of all to install. All you need is a convenient place to plug them in.

Heat exchangers and grates

A fan-driven heat exchanger or blower combines an airtight door with heat-exchanging tubes that wrap around the fire. A variable-speed blower draws in room air and returns the fire-heated air to the room. The unit fits into the existing firebox and can be adjusted with a trim kit to fit the opening snugly. Glass doors and a built-in fire screen allow a view of the fire. These units usually don't require a chimney liner, but check local building codes.

Grate heaters, or heat grates, work on the same general principle as heat exchangers: they draw in room air, circulate it through steel tubing, and send the warmed air back into the room. But instead of being sold as a complete package, they are offered as separate components (with or without a variable-speed fan) that can be combined with glass doors that you purchase separately.

Grate heaters are available for use with either wood or gas. At least one manufacturer offers a grate with a cast-iron heat reflector shield that radiates still more heat into the room.

VICTORIAN-STYLE GAS INSERT

WOOD-BURNING INSERT

Gas log sets

For use in a wood-burning masonry or prefab fireplace, a gas log set may be vented, ventless, or partially vented. Whichever type you choose, it should be installed by a professional plumber or heating contractor.

Vented logs look the most like a real wood fire; they produce a yellow flame and have glowing "embers," and they can be supplied with additional logs, branches, and even pine cones. The ceramic "logs" simulate oak, pine, or other woods; the grate they rest on looks like a regular wood-fire grate. These log sets must be used with the fireplace damper open, so they are not always the most efficient heaters.

GAS LOG SET

GAS LOG ASSEMBLY—LOGS, GRATE, BURNER, CINDERS, AND EMBERS

Ventless log sets look more realistic than they used to because a ventless yellow gas flame has replaced the old blue gas flame. Since ventless log sets can be used with the fireplace damper closed, they produce more heat than vented ones. But some locales don't allow them because of concerns about indoor air pollution. The sets do have an oxygen depletion sensor (ODS) to turn off the flame if oxygen levels drop too low. Still, it's best not to use them in a very tightly constructed home, or if someone living there is elderly or has respiratory problems.

The in-between choice is a partially vented log set that allows you to leave your damper slightly open. It won't put out as much heat as ventless logs, nor does it look as realistic as vented logs, but this is a viable compromise if allowed in your area.

Gas log sets include a single or dual burner that must be hooked up to a gas line. Additional materials such as silica sand, artificial cinders, and lava rocks that simulate chunks of burning wood may come with the set or be offered separately. Spread around the burner pan and fireplace floor, these give the fire a realistic look.

Log sets usually come with specific directions as to how they should be set up. The grate that holds the ceramic logs is placed over the burner pan and the logs are arranged on top, sometimes according to a specified pattern and sometimes according to user preference. When the fire is lit, the logs, lava rocks, and cinders actually absorb heat, take on a glow, and radiate warmth.

DUAL BURNER SYSTEM FOR GAS LOGS

LAVA ROCK "COALS"

CERAMIC-FIBER CINDERS AND EMBERS

Freestanding Stoves & Fireplaces

WARMING UP THE HOUSE IN STYLE

Several types of appliances fall into the broad general category of stand-alone heaters. The most popular are freestanding stoves fueled by wood, pellets, coal, gas, or electricity. These heat sources use modern technology to meet all EPA standards for clean burning. (For a comparison of fuels, see pages 120–121.) European freestanding fireplaces (also called masonry heaters, heat-storing fireplaces, or high-mass thermal heaters) are big, heavy soapstone appliances that also meet EPA standards and provide long-term radiant heat (see page 15). They may be fueled by wood, gas, or sometimes electricity.

Prefab freestanding wood-burning metal fireplaces are simple fireboxes with metal chimneys that may not meet EPA standards (see pages 17–18).

Freestanding stoves

Today's freestanding stoves come in a variety of attractive designs, both traditional and contemporary. Made of cast iron or steel, they often feature soapstone cladding or porcelain enamel finishes available in a rainbow of colors. Most have glass doors for fire-viewing. Styles range from sleek drum-shaped or cylindrical models to more traditional square or pot-bellied ones, with or without decorative panels and trim. European wood stoves are distinctly contemporary in style (see photo on facing page); they are often tall and cylindrical, made of steel and soapstone.

Wood-burning and gas-fired stoves require venting through a metal chimney; requirements will vary with the stove itself and with the configuration of your space. Some manufacturers offer chimneys in colored enamel finishes to match their stoves.

WOOD STOVE

WOOD STOVES. Among all wood-burning options, wood stoves offer the highest heating efficiency. New wood stoves *must* have the EPA-certified label (see page 25), showing that they meet standards for clean burning. To achieve this they may use either catalytic or noncatalytic technology (see page 19).

It's usually best to buy the highest-quality stove you can afford; look for good workmanship and solid construction. A firebrick lining can increase both the life of your stove and the amount of radiant heat it will produce. Also look for a stove with a special airflow system that keeps the glass doors clean.

Your dealer can help you determine what size stove you should choose, based on the area you want to heat. Keep in mind that the interior stove dimensions determine the size of wood you can burn.

HIGH-EFFICIENCY WOOD STOVE

EUROPEAN WOOD STOVE

Most wood stoves have features such as top or side loading, removable ash pans, insulated door handles, leg levelers, thermostats, and blower fans for increased heating. Optional extras may include spark screens that let you leave the stove doors open (when you're there) as well as stove-top steamers that you fill with water to humidify dry winter air. Other options are griddles and warming shelves for cooking on your stove and racks for drying wet mittens and socks.

Pellet stoves are highly efficient variations of wood-burning stoves that are neat and clean to operate. The pellets are fed into the stove automatically by an electrically powered auger system; most manufacturers offer battery backup operation. Pellet stoves are pictured on pages 18 and 83.

GAS STOVES. Looking much like their wood-burning counterparts, most gas stoves require venting through a metal chimney. Like manufactured gas fireplaces and inserts, gas stoves may be direct-vent, B-vent, or vent-free (see page 100). Most burn natural gas, but many offer a conversion kit for burning propane. At least one manufacturer offers a highly durable ceramic burner; most stoves feature steel tube burners.

Options available with a gas stove are nonelectric ignition systems, fans, wall thermostats, and remote controls. Although in many older models a high flame meant high heat, some stoves now vent out excess heat, so you can have high flames with less heat. You can even program ON and OFF times on some models.

ELECTRIC STOVE

COLOR-COORDINATED ENAMELED METAL CHIMNEYS

ELECTRIC STOVES. Electric stoves have all the same qualities, attributes, and drawbacks as their manufactured fireplace counterparts. They're clean, portable, and simple to operate—just plug in and enjoy. They require no venting or clearances from combustible surfaces, and they are being manufactured to look much like their wood- and gas-fired counterparts. Of course, their "flames" don't give you the same ambience as a real or even a gas fire, but they can be used everywhere, from a trailer to a tenth-story condo.

European fireplaces

Made of heavy soapstone that absorbs heat from a short, hot fire, free-standing European fireplaces radiate warmth gently into the room for 12 to 24 hours. Depending on their size, some models can heat up to 2,000 square feet. They may be vented from the sides, rear, or top through masonry, poured-in-place, or prefab chimneys.

These heaters, pictured on pages 15 and 82, feature clean-burning technology like that of wood stoves. Most have interior channels that circulate heat so it warms the fireplace walls. You can view the fire through glass doors on the firebox. Some feature bake ovens, too.

GAS STOVE WITH STONE HEARTH

Hearth pads

For safety, a wood stove must sit on a noncombustible base; the manufacturer's installation directions dictate how large this should be. The base can be a concrete slab (either bare or with a decorative surface of tile or brick), ceramic or stone tile on top of cement underlayment board, or a pre-fabricated stove board or mat. A stone slab of sufficient thickness is another option, as are floor plates of steel and even clear tempered glass.

The stove must also be a prescribed distance from any combustible wall, unless the wall is protected with a panel of brick, stone, or cement board, or with a stove shield. Your stove dealer can advise you as to what is needed for your situation.

Some pellet and gas stoves can be installed directly over any floor surface except linoleum and carpeting, while others require a hearth pad or floor plate. Some clearance from walls is usually required for stoves; check the manufacturer's installation directions.

Mantels & Surrounds

CREATING A DISTINCTIVE LOOK FOR YOUR FIREPLACE

When you choose materials and a style for your fireplace surround, or facing, you're making a strong design statement in your room. Whether you've selected a traditional masonry fireplace, a prefabricated model, or an insert, what gives it character are the mantel, facing, and hearth. From the simplest option—a plain mantel—to a full-blown stone mantel, surround, and hearth combination, you have numerous possibilities from which to make your choice. You'll see all kinds of mantels and facings illustrated in photos throughout this book.

A mantel is actually a decorative frame around the fireplace and its facing. The ledge above the firebox is the mantel shelf; the "legs" are the vertical elements on either side of the firebox. Sometimes an overmantel, a panel above the shelf, is part of the design. The surround (sometimes called the filler panel) is the frame right around the firebox; it must be of noncombustible material.

A mantel made of noncombustible materials can be built right up to the firebox opening without an intervening facing. For a wood mantel, check with your fire department and building code officials to see how close combustible materials can be to the firebox opening and how far a mantel shelf can project.

To explore your options, visit home improvement stores and fireplace and mantel dealers' showrooms. If you're seeking a vintage mantel, you'll want to haunt antique stores and salvage yards. Don't overlook the Internet (search under "Fireplace mantels") as a source of ideas.

CONCRETE WITH ROUGH-CUT GRANITE

Shelf mantels

The simplest of treatments, these "floating" mantels range from a single rough-hewn beam or a simple shelf on brackets to a fancy prefabricated mantel. You can install a shelf mantel directly on the wall above a firebox opening, whether the wall is constructed of drywall, stone, brick, or another material.

Full-surround mantels

Manufacturers of both prefabricated and made-to-order mantels offer mantel shelves, legs, and overmantels in mix-and-match options in a variety of designs. Legs may be simple, or they may be more elaborate pilasters or columns. You can purchase prefabs to fit around corner fireplaces as well as single-face fireplaces.

Off-the-shelf mantels offer a relatively inexpensive alternative to custom-made designs. Least expensive is unfinished paint-grade fiberboard; the most costly is stainable oak, cherry, or other hardwood or fruitwood. Designs range from plain and simple to intricately routed and trimmed.

Ready-made mantels come in various sizes, often adjustable to fit your particular fireplace and room. Prefab fireplace makers often offer ready-made mantels to fit their products. Some claim that these make it possible to have a new fireplace and mantel delivered and installed in less than a day's time.

If you want a one-of-a-kind mantel and surround tailored to your room and your fireplace, custom-made and site-built is the way to go. You'll have carte blanche in choosing your materials and designs—for a price.

*READY-MADE MANTEL
FOR PREFAB FIREPLACE*

RIVER ROCK WITH SHELF MANTEL OF RECYCLED WOOD

BRICK SURROUND WITH WOOD SHELF MANTEL

Material choices

Under most circumstances, you'll be choosing separate materials for mantel and facing. The latter must be a non-combustible material such as tile, brick, metal, cast concrete, or stone.

WOOD. For a truly classic-looking mantel, or for some rustic styles, wood is the top choice. The best wood mantels are like pieces of fine heirloom furniture—made of hardwood or fruitwood, beautifully stained and sealed with hand-rubbed finishes. They can be plain, adorned with simple decorative paneling and molding, or elaborately carved. A mantel of lower-grade hardwood or softwood can also be charming when painted—either a solid color or antiqued, distressed, or even painted with a faux-marble finish.

STONE AND ROCK. These are timeless, nearly indestructible materials for mantels and facings. A surround of natural rock must be constructed on-site by a mason. One alternative—cultured stone—allows you to have a natural rock look (actually a veneer) that weighs only about a quarter as much as natural stone.

If you don't want the rustic or "natural" look, consider a prefabricated or custom stone mantel of marble, granite, limestone, or slate—elegant if expensive. Among carved styles, the least costly are imported machine-carved marble mantels; hand-carved ones are true luxury items.

Cast stone replicates the look of hand-cut limestone. Cast limestone actually contains crushed limestone; less costly types of cast stone may not. Styles run the gamut from spare, clean-lined looks to mantels that appear ornately carved.

BRICK AND TILE. Brick is the longtime traditional facing for fireplaces, but a wide range of looks can be produced with it depending on what kind and color of bricks you use and what pattern you lay them in. Brick is heavy, so you may need extra structural support if you use a lot of it.

Versatile tile, either stone or ceramic, comes in nearly endless colors, finishes, and styles—from sleek polished granite squares to pebbly surfaced ceramics or charming blue and white Delft. For a contemporary look, install tiles as a wide facing only, without the surrounding mantel or even mantel shelf. Or use a tile facing within a full mantel surround. One manufacturer of gas fireplaces lets you change the tile for different looks: 4-by-4 tiles slip into a frame mounted to the drywall.

WOOD MANTEL WITH TILE SURROUND

METAL. Mantels and surrounds of metal may be historical reproductions or sleekly contemporary. A cast-bronze mantel in Victorian style may feature a hand-rubbed gold or verdigris finish. Cutting-edge styles—gleaming surrounds of rolled steel and even stainless steel tiles—must be custom-designed.

PLASTER AND GYPSUM. Poured in molds, plaster mantels tend to have a smooth finish. They can also have more intricate detailing than most carved-wood pieces, and you can paint the plaster to match your decor. Like plaster, glass fiber–reinforced gypsum offers ornate detailing achieved by casting in molds.

CONCRETE. Precast concrete mantels are great for achieving interesting custom looks because they may be finished in varied ways—from sandblasted to smooth to acid-washed—and come in a broad spectrum of colors. Cast in one piece or in modules, they are lightweight because they're reinforced with glass fiber.

Antique mantels

If your heart is set on a vintage mantel and you have the good luck to find an appropriate one of wood or stone, it can usually be adjusted to fit. (You'll probably wind up cutting down one that's too large.) Get professional help to determine how best to adapt your antique mantel according to building and fire codes.

Hearths

The hearth material usually matches that of the noncombustible fireplace facing—rock, stone, tile, brick, or concrete. Cast-in-place concrete is an appealing newer choice. Another option is a seamless stone slab installed as a hearth, applied with thinset mortar over a base of concrete.

Depending on the height of the fireplace on the wall, the hearth may be level with the floor or raised. A raised hearth can be extended out to provide seating or a footrest.

ANTIQUE CARRARA MARBLE MANTEL

Fireplace Accessories

FUNCTIONAL FINERY FOR YOUR FIREPLACE

HAND-FORGED LOUVERED IRON FRAME WITH MESH AND GLASS DOORS

Certain "extras" that you can add to your fireplace will contribute toward its output of heat and also add to its safety and its decorative appeal. Numerous other accessories, from pokers and tongs to match holders, can help you store fuel, kindle and manage a wood fire, and beautify your fireplace area all at the same time.

Shop for screens, firebacks, and grates at your local fireplace store, custom order them, or search on the Internet for "Fireplace accessories" or "Fire screens." Tools and other accessories can also be found at home improvement stores, stores specializing in forged iron, crafts fairs, and open studios; antique pieces are always a serendipitous find.

Fire screens

Glass doors, wire mesh fire curtains, and attached or freestanding glass or metal screens all share the same basic function: they provide protection from flying embers and safeguard children and pets. Glass doors also keep warmed air from escaping up the chimney.

GLASS DOORS. Made to fit neatly in a firebox opening, glass doors come in a variety of styles for traditional masonry fireplaces. (Some local and state regulations *require* glass doors for masonry fireplaces.) Most manu-facturers of prefab fireplaces offer doors with their units, and you can also purchase them separately.

If your fireplace has a standard-size opening, you can often buy arched or rectangular glass doors ready-made; otherwise you can have doors custom-made. The glass must be tempered; it may be clear, smoked, or tinted. The sturdiest frames are constructed of brass or steel (less expensive models may be aluminum). Frame finishes range from polished or antique brass to copper, nickel, or brushed steel.

Doors may be cabinet-style, bifold, or full-fold; models with no center bar give a clean, all-glass look and a full view of the fire. Some glass doors come with integral wire-mesh curtains, and some have top and bottom louvers for fire control.

FITTED WIRE-MESH SPARK GUARD

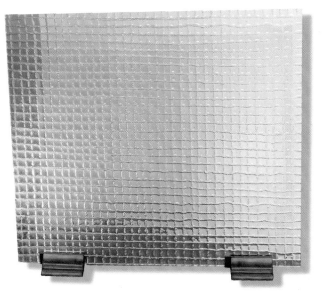

TEMPERED "BURLAP" GLASS SCREEN

HAND-POLISHED BRASS FREESTANDING SCREEN

MESH CURTAINS. Wire-mesh curtain screens installed on the top edge of the firebox opening keep sparks from flying out into the room. You pull them open and shut with a pull chain, like draperies. Mesh curtains should be made of heavy-gauge wire, and they should glide smoothly. They work best in tandem with glass doors, but you can install the curtains by themselves.

FREESTANDING SCREENS. The easiest fireplace option, screens don't usually need to be fitted—they just have to be big enough to cover the firebox opening. And a screen can be an important decorative accent as well as an effective barrier to sparks.

Ready-made or custom-crafted, fire screens come in a dazzling selection of designs and materials. You'll find hinged folding screens and single-piece standing screens on legs, in tempered glass or wire mesh, in styles ranging from ornate Victorian to Craftsman to minimalist contemporary.

Frames may be made of iron, steel, or cast brass. They should be heavy and stable. Sometimes you can find antique examples in good condition; just be sure they're the right size for your fireplace.

Firebacks

Decorative cast-iron panels designed to stand behind the fire, firebacks were once common in masonry fireplaces. They have become a lesser-known accessory in modern times— but, in fact, these freestanding pieces are practical as well as decorative. They absorb heat and radiate it back into the room while protecting the firebrick from soot and wear.

Firebacks are suitable for both wood-burning and gas log masonry fireplaces. Although you may have the good fortune to find an antique one that's in good condition (worn or damaged firebacks could be dangerous), you can now find new versions in stores and through the Internet. You can also find three-panel reflectors suitable for use behind gas logs.

ANTIQUE FIREBACK

Grates and andirons

A fire grate supports the logs in your fireplace and allows air to circulate underneath for better combustion. Ordinary grates are simply iron grids on legs. But beautiful, decorative grates are available in reproduction period styles as well as cutting-edge contemporary designs.

Buy the heaviest, most solidly built grate you can find and it will serve you for many years. Some grates can be used with gas fires; consult your fireplace dealer about them.

A time-honored alternative to a basket- or grid-style fire grate is a set of andirons, sometimes called firedogs. These L-shaped metal supports cradle logs laid across their horizontal bars. Vertical supports—usually highly decorative—keep the logs from rolling out onto the hearth. Look for antique sets as well as new styles.

BRASS ANDIRONS

FIRE GRATE

FORGED IRON RAM'S-HEAD ANDIRONS

FORGED IRON FENDER AND THREE-PANEL SCREEN

Fireplace tools

Purchased as separate pieces or as a matched set—often with its own stand—fireplace tools are essential to maintaining a well-burning wood fire. You'll need a poker for arranging burning logs and a pair of fireplace tongs for picking up pieces of wood. Also useful for cleaning out cold ashes from a spent fire are a long-handled shovel and brush.

You may choose tools that are handmade or mass-produced, of forged iron or solid brass, in a variety of finishes. You can even find antique tools, although some may look too beautiful to use! Buy the best you can afford, especially when it comes to tongs, which must be reliable. Consider buying a set of bellows, too; this simple, old-fashioned "tool" can wake up a dying fire with a few quick puffs of air.

WOOD STOVE TOOL SET

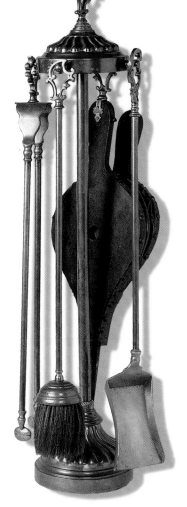

ANTIQUE FRENCH TOOL SET WITH BELLOWS

BRUSHED-NICKEL TOOLS AND STAND

BELLOWS

OPEN DOOR POLICY

Be sure to keep glass fireplace doors open while a fire is burning; a very hot fire could blow them out. Once the fire is out, the doors should be closed in order to keep warm room air from going up the chimney. It's a good idea to close them when the fire is smoldering and dying out, but the fireplace damper must stay open to let out gases and smoke.

Fenders

Also called "rails," fenders are essentially foot rests of brass, steel, or even wire, set on the hearth across the front of the firebox. In bygone days these were ubiquitous; people used them instead of screens to keep logs from rolling onto the hearth, to keep crawling babies out of the fire, and to protect ladies' long skirts.

Fenders can be quite decorative and lend a certain distinguished air to your fireplace. You can still find antique examples, but new ones are also being made, including reproductions of antique originals.

BRASS FENDER

SERPENTINE WIRE FENDER

Wood holders

You can find numerous styles of metal log cradles and racks for storing small amounts of firewood and kindling near your wood-burning fireplace or stove. U-shaped configurations take up the least space.

Some styles coordinate with fireplace tool sets or fire screens. Creative alternatives range from new or antique pails to old tubs, troughs, or boilers. Large baskets also make attractive log holders. For carrying wood in from the woodpile, you might want a canvas or leather sling as well.

FOLDING LEATHER LOG CARRIER

LOG CRADLE AND TOOL STAND

Other accessories

Among other fireplace accessories are metal damper plaques that tell you whether the damper is open or closed, cans or pails for carrying out cold ashes, and wall-mounted or free-standing match holders.

A fire-resistant hearth rug to protect your floor or carpet from sparks can be a useful and attractive addition to your fireplace area; wool is appropriate though expensive, while synthetic rugs treated with flame retardant are less costly.

Finally, if you have a fireplace with a gas starter, you can find fancy gas keys that look attractive hanging on a hook by your fireplace.

GAS KEYS

WALL-MOUNT MATCH HOLDER

BRASS MATCH HOLDERS

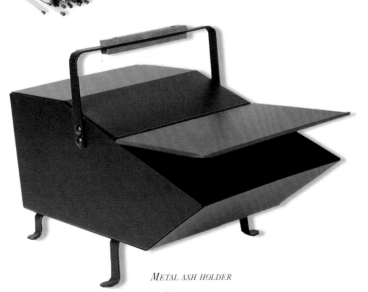

METAL ASH HOLDER

Fuel Choices

EXPLORING YOUR OPTIONS FOR STOVE AND FIREPLACE

The kind of fuel you wish to use—or are allowed to use in your area—is a crucial factor in deciding what kind of fireplace or stove to install. Consider availability and cost, heat efficiency, and both local and federal clean-air standards. Before making your choice, visit a reputable fireplace store to learn more, especially about community standards where you live.

Wood

The woodsy aroma, audible crackling and snapping, and mesmerizing flames of a wood fire can't be truly duplicated, but when considering

SPLIT LOGS

wood you must find out whether it is even allowed in your area. If you do burn wood, you will probably be required to have a fireplace or stove that meets EPA standards. To get the most out of firewood, building a hot and clean-burning fire is essential—see page 61.

Firewood is sold by the cord; a standard cord is a stack of split wood 4 feet high by 4 feet wide by 8 feet long. Look for suppliers in your phone directory under "Firewood," in the classified section of your local newspaper, or on the Internet.

Be sure to purchase split and seasoned wood, tightly stacked. Wood must be well seasoned to burn safely and efficiently, and usually all logs more than 6 inches in diameter should be split for faster seasoning. Split logs need to dry at least 6 to 12 months. (Note that the wood must fit into the firebox of your fireplace or wood stove, which may mean you'll have to split it further yourself.) Most suppliers will deliver the wood (usually for an added fee), but they won't stack it for you.

Be prepared to store your split logs in a dry spot outdoors where they will be convenient to carry in to your fireplace or stove. You'll also want an area indoors near the fireplace for small amounts.

Manufactured firelogs

Made of dry, fine-particle sawdust and wax, factory-formed "logs" burn slowly at high temperatures, reducing heat loss and pollution.

A "densified" log of compressed sawdust without the wax burns slowly and more cleanly than natural firewood; it's a good choice for wood-burning masonry or prefab fireplaces. Firelogs are not recommended for wood stoves.

Manufactured logs can be purchased in small numbers, so storage usually isn't a problem. However, they may cost more to use than natural wood.

PELLETS

Pellets

A relatively new fuel type, pellets are comprised of nuggets of compressed wood waste. Loaded into a hopper in the back of a specially designed stove or insert, they are fed to the firebox by a motor-driven auger at a controlled rate. Because pellets are a clean, compressed fuel, they are relatively easy to store and handle. Usually they are sold in 40- to 50-pound bags.

MANUFACTURED FIRELOGS

Natural gas

A highly desirable fuel option in many areas, natural gas is clean-burning and efficient. More and more prefab fireplaces and stoves are being designed to use it. Gas-fired appliances don't require buying or storing logs or pellets, and you can easily adjust flame height, heat output, and fire duration. In most communities, gas-burning appliances are not an issue from a clean-air standpoint; it's just a matter of whether you have a gas line.

In many areas, propane gas may be the only choice. Most gas appliances work equally well with propane, but check with the dealer to make sure.

Electricity

Electric fireplaces, inserts, and stoves are the easiest of all to install and maintain. All you need to plug them in is standard household current. Electricity is relatively inexpensive, and these appliances can go pretty much anywhere.

Coal

For stoves manufactured to burn coal or wood, this is a clean-burning option—but high-grade fuel coal isn't readily available everywhere. The best grade for home heating is anthracite, or "hard coal"; varieties mined in eastern Pennsylvania are the most desirable. Coal is sold by the ton and delivered to your home.

Gel fuel

Much like the alcohol fuel used to warm buffet dishes, gel fuel comes in small canisters that burn for two or three hours. Look for gel fuel in home centers and hardware stores or where portable outdoor fireplaces are sold.

You can use this fuel for occasional fires in specially designed freestanding "fireplaces" that require no vent, so they can go virtually anywhere except bedrooms. However, such fireplaces are definitely for short-term use, in well-ventilated rooms or outdoors.

STACKING AND STORING FIREWOOD

Split firewood should be stacked off the ground to keep it dry. It can be laid atop concrete blocks, old pieces of lumber, or even old wood pallets, if you can find them, and it should be loosely covered to keep out dew and rain yet still let air circulate. Try to locate your wood in a sunny, well-ventilated area away from house walls, since woodpiles are often hosts to termites and other pests.

If you don't have a roofed woodshed, you can make a storage frame from 2 by 4s and special metal brackets purchased at a home improvement store, hardware store, or lumberyard. A plastic tarp can be used to cover the woodpile.

To stack firewood properly, use one of the two configurations shown here. Another good way to build a woodpile is to use the crisscross method for the end stacks and then fill in between them using the parallel method. Either way, place pieces bark side up; bark repels water better than the interior wood does.

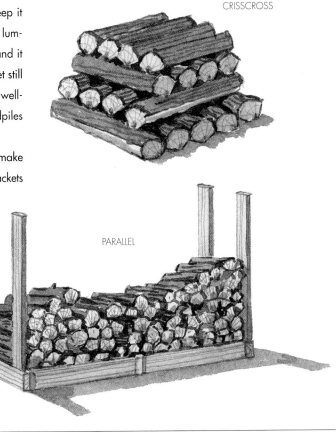

CRISSCROSS

PARALLEL

Portable Outdoor Fireplaces

MINI-FIREPLACES FOR DECK OR PATIO

Fun and practical additions to your patio or backyard, little portable fire pits and chiminea fireplaces are sold in home and garden stores, through catalogs, and on the Internet. They can add warmth and ambience to your backyard, and with the addition of a grill some can be used for barbecuing.

In a cold-winter or rainy climate, you will need to store your portable fireplace in a protected indoor area such as a carport, garage, or basement.

Fire pits

Freestanding metal fire pits are often decorative as well as practical backyard assets, featuring sleek designs or even fanciful cutouts in their sides. They are available in a choice of wood-burning, propane gas–fueled, or gel alcohol versions.

Wood- or charcoal-burning fire pits come in a variety of designs, from wide and shallow copper basins on steel legs to three-legged, drum-shaped open pits of high-carbon steel. Some mesh-walled "drums" rest on tall legs with wheels.

Most portable fire pits have a sturdy wire-mesh spark screen for safety; mesh-walled models are designed with an access door. Some kettle-shaped types feature a ring of heavy steel that serves as a footrest. You can add an optional grill to some models.

Fire pits fueled by gel alcohol are glass-enclosed. Often shaped like large lanterns, they come in aluminum, stainless steel, and even copper.

The high-carbon steel fire pit at left has a heavy steel foot rest that doubles as a handle. At right, a handsome copper basin on a wrought-iron stand has a domed spark screen that swings open for adding firewood—or toasting marshmallows. Both fire pits are equipped with optional grills.

Chimineas

The three-legged clay chiminea has
become a popular outdoor mini-
fireplace. Its characteristic little chimney may be integral to the squat base
or sold as a separate piece. You can
find chimineas in unadorned terra-
cotta or in more decorative finishes
and colors. Besides the traditional
clay, chimineas of cast iron, aluminum,
steel, and copper are also sold.

These charmers range widely
in price and quality; buy from a reputable dealer to ensure that yours
is properly fired to withstand heat.
Most chimineas also need to be
weather-sealed.

Chimineas—most of which are
made for fire-watching and not for
cooking—may burn wood or miniature
manufactured logs made expressly
for them. Some can be used with
gas-log sets. Consult the dealer or
the manufacturer's instructions for
instructions on how to "cure" a
wood-burning chiminea before first
use and how to insulate the bowl
with sand or gravel.

Accessories for chimineas can be
purchased separately at home and garden centers. Along with spark screens
and heatproof mats (for use on decks),
you'll find protective covers, firewood
holders, tool sets, and even candle
holders that sit inside the bowl when
you're seeking atmosphere more than
actual warmth.

*This one-piece chiminea has its own
spark screen and stand, as well as
a handle encircling the chimney.*

resources

The following listing of manufacturers, dealers' showrooms, and general information sources is a good place to begin your search for the fireplace or stove that's right for you. Here you'll find a sampling of the wide range of products available to you, from modern prefab fireplaces to antique mantels, from European stoves to portable outdoor fire pits. Internet sites can be excellent places to learn about different types of fireplaces and stoves, and their installation requirements, before visiting retail showrooms to see a variety of models close at hand.

Fireplaces & stoves/ related products

A & M Victorian Decorations, Inc.
2411 Chico Ave.
South El Monte, CA 91733
(800) 671-0693
www.aandmvictorian.com
Cast stone, metal, wood, and marble mantels

A Plus
151 DeKalb Industrial Way
Decatur, GA 30030-2201
(404) 373-7587
www.aaplusinc.com
Plaster mantels, fireplace systems

Adobelite
10031 Southern SE
Albuquerque, NM 87123
(505) 291-0500
www.adobelite.com
Prefab lightweight kiva-style fireplaces

ArcusStone
5601 San Leandro St.
Oakland, CA 94621
(510) 535-9300
www.ArcusStone.com
Crushed-limestone coatings and plasters

Ball and Ball Antique Hardware Reproductions
463 W. Lincoln Hwy.
Exton, PA 19341
(800) 257-3711
www.ballandball-us.com
Fireplace fenders and other reproduction antique hardware

Balmer Studios
271 Yorkland Rd.
Toronto, Ontario
Canada M2J 1S5
(416) 491-6425
www.balmerstudios.com
Glass fiber–reinforced gypsum mantels

Buckley Rumford Fireplaces
1035 Monroe St.
Port Townsend, WA 98368
(360) 385-9974
www.rumford.com
Rumford fireplaces, related products

CJ's HomeDecor + Fireplaces
7 Ilene Court, Unit 18
Hillsborough, NJ 08844
(877) 373-6677
www.fireplacenclosures.com
Glass fireplace doors, grate heaters, heat exchangers

Collinswood Designs
1400 Duff Dr.
Fort Collins, CO 80524
(800) 482-1464
www.collinswooddesigns.com
Hardwood mantels, related cabinetry

Concrete Designs
3650 S. Broadmont Dr.
Tucson, AZ 85713
(800) 279-2278
www.concrete-designs.com
Concrete mantels

Cultured Stone
PO Box 270
Napa, CA 94559-0270
(800) 255-1727
www.culturedstone.com
Manufactured stone veneers

Dogpaw Design
1416 N.W. 51st Street
Seattle, WA 98117
(206) 706-0099
www.dogpaw.com
Custom pre-cast architectural concrete

The Firebird
1808 Espinacitas St.
Santa Fe, NM 87505
(505) 983-5264
www.thefirebird.com
Prefab fireplaces, inserts, stoves, accessories

Fireplace Antique Store
(800) 258-7444
www.fireplaceantiquestore.com
Antique fireplace surrounds, accessories

Fireplace Xtrordinair/ Travis Industries
10850 117th Place NE
Kirkland, WA 98033
www.fireplacextrordinair.com
Wood-burning and gas prefab fireplaces

Fires of Tradition
17 Passmore Crescent
Brantford, Ontario
Canada N3T 5L6
(519) 770-0063
www.firesoftradition.com
Antique reproduction surrounds and mantels, fire grates, electric and gas fireplaces

FoxFire
760 S. Auburn St.
Grass Valley, CA 95945
(530) 272-1878
www.foxfirestoves.com
Prefab fireplaces, stoves, related products

Grand Mantel
(888) 473-9663
www.GrandMantel.com
Ready-made and customized wood mantels, hearths, cabinetry

The Hearth Collection
(310) 323-6720
www.hearthcollection.com
Heirloom-quality fireplace screens, accessories

Hearthlink
9 Maple St.
Randolph, VT 05060
(877) 337-8414
www.outdoorfireplaces.com
Chimineas, fire pits, other outdoor fireplaces

HearthStone
317 Stafford Ave.
Morrisville, VT 05661
(800) 827-8603
www.hearthstonestoves.com
Wood and gas stoves

Heatilator/Hearth Technologies, Inc.
1915 West Saunders St.
Mt. Pleasant, IA 52641
(800) 927-6841
www.heatilator.com
Prefab wood-burning and gas fireplaces

Heat-N-Glo
20802 Kensington Blvd.
Lakeville, MN 55044
(888) 427-3973
www.heatnglo.com
Gas and wood-burning prefab fireplaces

Isokern Fireplace Systems/ Earthcore Industries
6899 Phillips Industrial Blvd.
Jacksonville, FL 32256
(800) 642-2920
www.isokern.net
Precast modular fireplaces

Jøtul North America
400 Riverside St./PO Box 1157
Portland, ME 04104
(207) 797-5912
www.jotulflame.com
Norwegian cast-iron stoves, inserts, prefab fireplaces

K & W Manufacturing Co., Inc
23107 Temescal Canyon Rd.
Corona, CA 92883-5054
(909) 277-3300
www.k-and-w-mfg.com
FireMagic heat-circulating fireplaces

Kozy Heat
(800) 253-4904
www.kozyheat.com
Prefab gas fireplaces for indoors and outdoors

**Lennox Hearth Products/
Superior Products**
1110 West Taft Ave.
Orange, CA 92865
(800) 953-6669
www.lennoxhearthproducts.com
Prefab fireplaces, inserts, stoves, gas log sets, chimneys

Malm Fireplaces, Inc.
368 Yolanda Ave.
Santa Rosa, CA 95404
(707) 523-7755
www.malmfireplaces.com
Freestanding fireplaces

Mazzeo's Stoves & Fireplaces
Route 90, Farwell Dr./PO Box 232
Rockport, ME 04841
(207) 596-6496
www.mazzeosinc.com
Prefab fireplaces, inserts, stoves, accessories, chimney maintenance and restoration

Moburg Fireplaces
223 NW 9th Ave.
Portland, OR 97209
(503) 227-0547
www.modernrumford.com
Kit systems for building contemporary Rumford fireplaces

Okell's Fireplace
1300 17th St.
San Francisco, CA 94107
(415) 626-1110
www.okells.com
Prefab fireplaces, inserts, stoves, mantels and surrounds, tools, accessories

Old World Stoneworks
5400 Miller Ave.
Dallas, TX 75206
(800) 600-8336
www.oldworldstoneworks.com
Cast stone mantels

Pilgrim Fireplace Equipment Co.
2400 Cordelia Rd.
Fairfield, CA 94534
www.pilgrimhearth.com
Fireplace accessories

**Portland Willamette Distinctive
Fireplace Furnishings**
6800 NE 59th Place
Portland, OR 97218
(503) 288-7511
www.portwill.com
Glass fireplace doors, screens, gas log sets

Quadra-Fire/Aladdin Hearth Products
1445 North Hwy.
Colville, WA 99114
(800) 234-2508
www.aladdinhearth.com
Fireplaces, inserts, stoves, accessories, mantels, surrounds

Rais/Rais & Wittus, Inc.
40 Westchester Ave.
Pound Ridge, NY 10576
(914) 764-5679
www.raiswittus.com
Modern Scandinavian wood stoves, inserts

Raytech, Inc.
222 Fashion Lane #111
Tustin, CA 92780
(800) 838-5898
www.raytechstore.com
Prefab fireplaces, inserts, stoves, fireplace doors and accessories, patio heaters

Regency Fireplace Products
www.regency-fire.com
www.regencyshowcase.com
Prefab gas and wood-burning fireplaces, inserts, stoves, ready-made mantels

SCAN AMERICA
8111 NE Columbia Blvd.
Portland, OR 97218
(866) 722-6089
www.warmfurniture.com
Scandinavian wood stoves and soapstone freestanding fireplaces

Security Chimneys International Ltd.
2125 Monterey, Laval (Quebec)
Canada H7L 3T6
(450) 973-9999
www./securitychimneys.com
Prefab wood-burning fireplaces, chimneys, vents

SOJOE Firepits
PO Box 15359
San Luis Obispo, CA 93406
(888) 316-1404
www.sojoe.com
Freestanding outdoor fireplaces, fire pits

Stone Manufacturing Company
(310) 323-6720
www.stonemfg.com
Fireplace accessories

Temco Fireplace Products
1324 McArthur Dr.
Manchester, TN 37355
(800) 753-7736
1189 Iowa Ave.
Riverside, CA 92507
(909) 779-6766
www.temcofireplaces.com
Prefab fireplaces

Thelin Co. Inc.
12400 Loma Rica Dr.
Grass Valley, CA 95945
(530) 273-1976, (800) 949-5048
www.thelinco.com
Pellet and gas stoves

Tulikivi U.S., Inc.
One Penn Plaza, Suite 3600
New York, NY 10119
(212) 896-3897
www.tulikivi.com
European soapstone masonry heaters

Valor Radiant Gas Fireplaces
www.valorfireplaces.com
Prefab gas fireplaces

Vermont Castings/Majestic Products
410 Admiral Blvd.
Mississauga, Ontario
Canada L5T 2N6
(905) 670-7777
www.vermontcastings.com
www.majesticproducts.com
Wood and gas stoves, prefab fireplaces, inserts

Waterloo Gas Products
25 Northfield Dr. West
Waterloo, Ontario
Canada N2L 4E6
(519) 725-0196
www.waterloogasproducts.ca
Gas fireplaces and inserts, freestanding metal outdoor fireplaces and fire pits

Waterford Irish Stoves
www.waterfordstoves.com
Porcelain-enamel wood stoves, prefab wood-burning and gas fireplaces

Wilkening Fireplace Co.
9608 State 371 NW
Walker, MN 56484
(800) 367-7976
www.wilkeningfireplace.com
Heat exchangers, prefab fireplaces, inserts

Woodland Stoves & Fireplaces
1203 Washington Ave. South
Minneapolis, MN 55415
(612) 338-6606
www.woodlandstoves.com
Prefab fireplaces, inserts, stoves, European masonry heaters, accessories

Information/services

Chimney Safety Institute of America
2155 Commercial Dr.
Plainfield, IN 46168
(800) 536-0118
www.csia.org
General information, listing of CSIA-certified chimney sweeps

Environmental Protection Agency
1200 Pennsylvania Ave. NW
Washington, DC 20460
(202) 272-0167
www.epa.gov
Guidelines for reducing combustion pollutants

Hearth, Patio & Barbecue Assoc.
1601 North Kent St., Suite 1001
Arlington, VA 22209
(703) 522-0086
www.hpba.org
Basic information on fireplace and stove options, safety

The Irish Sweep
1400 Webster St., Suite 304
Alameda, CA 94501
(510) 521-4088
www.theirishsweep.com
General information, maintenance services

**Masonry Heater Association
of North America**
1252 Stock Farm Rd.
Randolf, VT 05060
(802) 728-5896
www.mha-net.org
Basic information, dealer directory

Pellet Fuels Institute
1601 N. Kent St., Suite 1001
Arlington, VA 22209
(703) 522-6778
www.pelletheat.org
Information about pellet stoves and fuel

The Wood Heat Organization
www.woodheat.org
Information on heating with wood

design &
photography
credits

design

FRONT MATTER

1 Architect: Philip Matthews and Jonathan Feldman, project manager/Philip Matthews Architect **2** Interior design: Linda Applewhite/Linda Applewhite & Associates

ALL KINDS OF HEARTHS

4 top Screen: Century Screens **4 bottom** Fireplace design: Wendle Schoniger/The August Company; Builder: Duane Heil **5** Architect: Robert Remiker; Interior design: Sarita Patel

PLANNING & DESIGN

6–7 Architect: Josh Chandler **7 small photo** Fireplace design: Lew French **8 bottom** Architect: Nasrin A. Barbee **9** Architect: Edward W. Buchanan/Jarvis Architects **10** Architect: Mark Moran/Tony Rosas Associates; Stove: SCAN 5 by SCAN AMERICA **11 top** Interior design: Nancy Gilbert/San Anselmo Country Store **12 bottom** Fireplace design: Jon Fredericks/Dogpaw Design **13** Interior design: Linda Applewhite/Linda Applewhite & Associates **15** Freestanding fireplace: KOJO by SCAN AMERICA **17** Fireplace: Malm Fireplaces **18 top** Pellet stove: Thelin Co. Inc. **18 bottom** Design: Thomassen Construction, Inc.; Propane stove: Lopi/Travis Industries **20** Design: Martyn Lawrence Bullard/Martynus Tripp **21 top** Andirons: Stone Manufacturing Company **21 bottom**

Architect: Mark Hutker and Associates, Architects **22 top** Tile: Fireclay Tile **23 top** Fireplace design: Jon Fredericks/Dogpaw Design **23 bottom** Mantel: Renaissance Company **24 top** Interior design: Janna Lund Rogers **24 bottom** Interior design: Elizabeth Hill/Selby House **25 top** Interior design: Kathryne Designs **26 bottom** Interior design: Bethe Cohen Design Associates for Sunset Idea House 2003; Fireplace construction: DeMattei Construction; Fireplace: Lennox Hearth Products **28 bottom** Architect: Philip Matthews and Jonathan Feldman, project manager/Philip Matthews Architect **31 top** Interior design: Ann Bertelsen and Leanne Holder for Sunset Idea House 2003 **31 bottom** Architect: Hawtin-Jorgenson Architects **32 top** Gloves: L.L. Bean **32 bottom** Landscape architect: David Fox; Fire screen sculptor: LMNO Arts **33** Design: Nicki Moffat

A GALLERY OF IDEAS

34–35 Architect: Mark Becker; Interior design: Tami Becker **36 bottom** Interior design: Linda Applewhite/Linda Applewhite & Associates **37 top** Fireplace design: Wendle Schoniger/The August Company; Builder: Duane Heil **37 bottom** Interior design: Linda Applewhite/Linda Applewhite & Associates **38 top** Interior design: Sarita Patel **38 bottom** Architect: Edward W. Buchanan/Jarvis Architects; Builder: S. C. Summerwood **39** Design: Glen Jarvis/Jarvis Architects **40** Architect:

Mark Becker; Interior designer: Tami Becker **41 top** Fireplace design: Wendle Schoniger/The August Company; Builder: Duane Heil **41 bottom** Architect: Philip Matthews and Jonathan Feldman, project manager/Philip Matthews Architect **42 left** Design: Bethany Opalach/Jarvis Architects; Builder: S. C. Summerwood **43** Interior design: Linda Applewhite/Linda Applewhite & Associates; Fireplace screen: Brian Kennedy **44 and 45 bottom** Architect: Dennis O'Connor; Interior designer: Elizabeth Hill/Selby House; Builder: Dan Singleton/Colorado Co. **44** Plaster work: Leo Murphy **45 top** Design: Jonathan Feldman/Jonathan Feldman Architecture **45 bottom** Architect: Dennis O'Connor; Interior designer: Elizabeth Hill/Selby House; Woodwork: Tom Shea and Bob Shook **46 top** Architect: Jarvis Architects **46 bottom** Architect: Robert Remiker; Interior designer: Sarita Patel **47** Architect: Edward W. Buchanan/Jarvis Architects **48 top** Fireplace design: Wendle Schoniger/The August Company; Builder: Duane Heil **48 bottom** Fireplace design: Todd Betts for ArcusStone **49 top** Fireplace design: Todd Betts/Betts Art **49 bottom** Interior design: Nancy Van Natta/Nancy Van Natta Associates **50 top** Interior design: Linda Applewhite/Linda Applewhite & Associates **52 top** Tool set: Stone Manufacturing Company **52 bottom** Fireplace: Fireplace Xtrordinaire/Travis Industries **53 top** Interior design: Charles De Lisle for San Francisco Decorator Showcase; Fireplace: Bendheim **55 top** Architect:

Thayer Hopkins/Thayer Hopkins Architects **55 bottom** Architect: Jim Somes **56 top** Design: Gordana Pavlović/Design Studio Gordana **56 bottom** Interior design: Stephen Sanborn **57** Architect: Jim Orjala/Orjala Architects **58** Fireplace design: Counter Production of Berkeley; Interior design: Bethe Cohen Design Associates for Sunset Idea House 2003; Construction: De Mattei Construction; Fireplace: Lennox Hearth Products **59 top** Design/construction: Ron and Peggy Roloff; Fireplace: Fireplace Xtraordinaire/Travis Industries **59 bottom** Interior design: Ann Bertelsen and Leanne Holder for Sunset Idea House 2003; Construction: De Mattei Construction; Fireplace: Lennox Hearth Products **60 top** Design: David Stark Wilson/Wilson Associates **60 bottom** Architect: David Trachtenberg/Trachtenberg Architects **61** Design: Barbara Barry **63 top** Tuscan grill: The Gardener **63 bottom** Interior design: Shirley Jensen/Forget-me-Nots Design; Construction: Dru Jensen **64 top** Design: Gordana Pavlovic/Design Studio Gordana **64 bottom** Architect: John Martin **65** Design: Martyn Lawrence Bullard/Martynus Tripp **66** Architect: Quigley Architects **67 top** Design: David Stark Wilson/Wilson Associates **68 bottom** Architect: Josh Chandler **69 top** Architect: Steven Ehrlich **69 bottom** Design: Jane Antonacci/Jane Antonacci and Associates **71 top** Design: Antine Associates **72 top** Architects: Virginia Schutte and Ken Hayes **72 bottom** Architect: Charles Rose; General contractor:

photography

If not otherwise credited, photographs are by **Jamie Hadley**.

index

Numbers in **boldface type** refer to photographs or drawings.